FEMINISM

And The Creation of a Female Aristocracy

By Peter Wright

Academic Century Press
2017

Table of Contents

Introduction

When Marxist activist Rudi Dutschke looked at ways to stage a neo-Marxist revolution he hit on the plan of "a long march through the institutions of power to create radical change from within government and society by becoming an integral part of the machinery." His strategy was to work against the established institutions while working surreptitiously within them. Evidence of the attempt to implement his plan can be seen today through many levels of society – especially in universities.

Marxists however are not the only ones to use this strategy. In fact when we look at the numerous political forces attempting to infiltrate and influence our cultural institutions we see that another, much more influential candidate, has twisted its tendrils through every layer of society – and it existed long before Marx and Marxism was born. That force is *political feminism*,[1] whose culture project has been in play now for several hundred years.

Protofeminists like Lucrezia Marinella, Mary Wollstoncraft, Margaret Cavendish, Modesta Pozzo, or Christine de Pizan were advocating a 'long march' through institutions for centuries before Marxism emerged and began its tragic experiment. Pizan's main book for example titled *'A City of Ladies'* sketched an imaginary city whose institutions were controlled completely by women, and each of the protofeminists advanced some theory of female rule or 'integration' of women into governing institutions.

A survey of these writings reveals that early protofeminists advocated the superior abilities of women as functionaries: women's greater virtue, nonviolence, intelligence, patience, superior morality and so on, combined with concomitant descriptions of male inferiority just as we see continued in the rhetoric of modern feminists. They sought not only a big slice of the pie, but as contemporary feminists have shown they would stop at nothing but the whole pie; nothing but complete dominance of the gendered landscape would satisfy their lust for control.

Feminists not only govern the modern world via their occupancy of pivotal bureaucratic positions, but such governance fails to resemble the utopia promised by early feminists; certainly not the utopic social order characterized by 'loving, egalitarian, and art-loving peoples free from war, conflict, and sexist domination.'

The behaviour of feminist-inspired functionaries is characterized by the destructive practices of "administrative discretion" which refers to the flexible exercise of decision-making allowed to public administrators. Such discretionary opportunity is made available by the wiggle-room in the bureaucrat's code of practice, and she or he uses that to deliver preferred, and often unfair, outcomes.

The use of administrative discretion typifies the *modus operandi* of all governance feminists, which is (mis)used to implement a radical feminist agenda through all levels of society. Feminism-inspired women are increasingly dominating HR roles, and as revealed by hiring biases at educational institutions, or government departments and businesses, they are exploiting that administrative discretion to favor females over males.

This development was already witnessed by early supporters of Men's Rights Movement who noted with concern that women seeking employment in key bureaucratic positions were misusing the positions they held. In 1948, for example, the British Men's Review remarked,

> "Women have captured practically intact the entire secretarial sphere. The communication gateway through which all letters must pass to reach those that control, whose actions can make or mar their fellow creatures lives. The possibilities with which this situation is pregnant requires but little imagination."[2]

That long tradition underlines the danger of viewing 'the march through the institutions' as a Cultural Marxism project alone, because it deflects from the historically longer, more powerful, more dangerous and ultimately more successful project that is political feminism.

Moreover, the protagonists of Marxist and feminist worldviews are not one and the same; the former aims to dismantle social-class oppression, and the latter gender oppression. While there are some individuals working to amalgamate these two contrary theories into a hybrid of Frankenstein proportions, their basic theoretical aims remain distinct.

Like Marxism, feminism too can be imagined as a socio-political ideology, in this case modelling itself on a medieval feudalism which was structured with a ruling King or Queen overseeing two social classes: 1. A noble class of aristocrats, priests, princes and princesses, and 2. a peasant class of serfs and slaves overseen by indentured vassals.

Stripped of its medieval context we see the purveyors of political feminism working to institute a sex stratified version of feudalism which serves to consolidate and increase the power of women. As with the peasant class in medieval times, the assets and wealth generated by the labour class – predominately men – are to be systematically taxed and redistributed to "aristocratic" women via a plethora of social, medical and occupational spending programs of governments, and in the form of asset transfers like alimony, child support, divorce settlements and other court mandated conventions. Children themselves form part of that asset portfolio which men are often forced to relinquish to women in the event of divorce.

The attempt to establish a quasi-aristocratic class comprised only of women has long been recognized, as mentioned by the following individual who in the year 1896 observed the granting to women of unequal social privileges; "It gives cause to some reflection" the author states, "as to the rate at which a sex aristocracy is being established in our midst."[3]

Adam Kostakis gives an eloquent summary of feminism's preference for a neo-feudal society in his seminal *Gynocentrism Theory Lectures*[4]:

"It would not be inappropriate to call such a system sexual feudalism, and every time I read a feminist article, this is the impression that I get: that they aim to construct a new aristocracy, comprised only of women, while men stand at the gate, till in the fields, fight in their armies, and grovel at their feet for starvation wages. All feminist innovation and legislation creates new rights for women and new duties for men; thus it tends towards the creation of a male underclass."[5]

By all accounts what we have today under feminist modelling is a successful attempt to establish a neo-feudal society with women representing an aristocratic class and men the labour class of serfs, slaves and peasants who too often spend their lives looking up from the proverbial glass cellar. This enterprise is 800 years in the making, enjoying consolidations with each and every passing year of feminist governance.

With this sombre overview of the state of play, we can now dive in and look at the internal mechanics of feminism as displayed in the contemporary movement. The following articles were previously published at Gynocentrism.com and have been updated for this volume. There are some minor repetition of quotes for which I ask the reader's grace – they are integral to the structure of the articles and for that purpose have been retained.

Chapters 1 – 5, featuring articles by Adam Kostakis, Ernest B. Bax, and Peter Wright provide pithy summaries of the feminist project and the historical roots of the movement. Chapters 6 – 7 take up the politics of beauty, followed by chapters 8 – 11 which deconstruct the internal rationale of feminist rhetoric.[6]

With much of this volume highlighting feminism's reliance on male chivalry, chapter 12 throws down the gauntlet and asks why chivalry needs to be a sexist convention at all, followed by chapter 13 which explores the possibility of relationships built on non-feminist, libertarian principles. Finally, chapter 14 reviews the 1971 pulp fiction book *The Feminists*, which concludes with the suggestion that a defeat of feminism can only come about when sufficient numbers of women join to oppose and fight it.

[1]. Ernest Belfort Bax coined the phrase 'political feminism' in his book *The Fraud of Feminism*. London: Grant Richards Ltd, 1913
[2] *The Men's Review*, London 1948
[3]. *A Privileged and Pampered Sex*, Letter to the Editor, Reynolds Newspaper, 1896
[4]. Adam Kostakis, Gynocentrism Theory Lectures, 2011 (https://gynocentrism.com/2014/05/25/gynocentrism-theory-2/)
[5]. Lecture 11: The Eventual Outcome of Feminism –II, *Gynocentrism Theory Lectures*, 2011
[6] Chapter 10 *Feminism's love-affair with gender differences* was co-authored by Bryan Scandrett, Robert Brockway and Peter Wright

What is feminism?

From every side of the gender debate people offer differing definitions of what 'feminism' is, with feminists themselves pointing to glib dictionary definitions, and antifeminists defining it as a female supremacy movement. Considering the hundreds of definitions circulating on the internet a more important question is whether these divergent definitions hold anything in common?

In the following excerpt Adam Kostakis answers this question in the affirmative with an elegant definition that most stakeholders would agree with.

Even *essentially contested concepts,* as W. B. Gallie referred to them, must have meanings which are *greater than normative,* else communication about them would be rendered impossible. That is – there must be some amount of general consensus over what feminism is, between feminists and anti-feminists, or we would not be able to argue about it! Even despite the differences between a feminist's view of feminism and of our own, some *shared content* must exist at some level, or we would be talking about entirely different things. They might be talking about the feminist movement, while I am talking about horse-rearing, although we both refer to our respective subjects as 'feminism' – but we wouldn't have much to say to each other, would we, if this were the case?

So, I shall posit the following as a *universally applicable* definition of feminism; that is to say, it must fit everyone's criteria for what feminism is, *in spite* of the different perspectives that different people hold on its nature. It is a suitably limited definition, since it can encompass only those parts of feminism which all definitions hold in common. So, here it is: **feminism is the project for increasing the power of women.**

That, then, is what everybody who discusses feminism holds in common regarding the concept, whether they are supportive, skeptical, or nihilistically indifferent. No feminist, I think, would deny that this is, at the very least, the 'bare bones' of feminism, even if she would prefer to flesh it out in a lot more detail. But that will not do, for beyond this narrow inference, *we disagree with each other.* To be as objective as possible, then, we must take only that which everybody agrees upon, and that is our universally applicable definition.

Note that there is no mention of equality. This is because there are a number of feminists who explicitly did not pursue equality, but supremacy. So, equality cannot fit into the universal definition of feminism, since certain feminists themselves – who were very famously, unequivocally feminist – disavowed it. To say that feminism is 'about equality', then, would be to place oneself in diametrical opposition to several extremely influential feminists! And why, that would be … *misogynistic!*

Nor can feminism be said to be the project for increasing the power of women *relative to men,* since, in this counter-feminist's view, feminists are often quite content to increase the power of women in an absolute sense. That is, they endeavor to *grab all they can* for women, without reference to the status of men. The phrase 'relative to men,' then, only serves to imply that women are power-*less* relative to men at present, thus casting feminism in an unfairly favorable light. In reality, once women do achieve power which is at an equal or equivalent level to that of men, the demands of feminists do not stop. What we find is that female power becomes entrenched, and extended, and when it surpasses male power, this is simply referred to as 'parity' and ignored by feminists – at least, when they are not gloating over men's newfound powerlessness.

Nor are we able to list, in our universal definition, the specific areas of life, or *spheres,* in which the feminist project applies. This is because feminism is inherently universalizing; it seeks to colonize and dominate every single facet of life where men and women meet. It aims for domination in *every* sphere of life, actual and potential.

You may disagree with some of the points above, particularly if you are supportive of feminism. But this does nothing to change our universal definition, because all we can say about those points is that *they are contentious.* That is, feminists and non-feminists, who are educated about feminism, disagree about these aspects of feminism, and it would simply be biased to take one or the other view for granted. That would be like consulting *only* Jacobins on the historical accomplishments of the Jacobin Club, or like canvassing *only* conservatives to explain modern liberalism. It would be a good example of poor methodology, and would help us very little in our search for truth. Right? So then, our universally applicable definition cannot be expanded beyond that which we stated before: **feminism is the project for increasing the power of women.**

Source: Adam Kostakis' *Pig Latin*, Lecture 4 of Gynocentrism Theory Lectures, 2011

Governance Feminism: a review

"The long march through the institutions is complete and feminists now occupy pivotal positions of power and decision-making throughout the world."

Despite being a feminist-friendly book with some of the usual agitprop, _Governance Feminism: An Introduction_[1] caught my eye because I have never seen an overt discussion of feminist institutional power by a feminist. It's a topic classified taboo for academics and authors despite the effects of that power being experienced by peoples around the planet daily .

The book intrigued and perhaps even excited me for the prospect that a veil of denial and secrecy surrounding feminist power might be perforated for the first time.

The four authors of the work dubbed their topic Governance Feminism (GF), by which they mean "every form in which feminists and feminist ideas exert a governing will within human affairs." This definition follows Michel Foucault's definition of governmentality in which feminists and feminist ideas "conduct the conduct of men." Governance Feminism is proposed as a new phrase, but it deserves mentioning that MRAs have been using the synonymous phrase 'Feminist Governance' for many years.

The work looks at feminist infiltration into positions of institutional and cultural power – the long march through the institutions that so many of us have been monitoring. Feminists have infiltrated the UN, World Bank, International Criminal Court, every layer of national governments, and further into universities, schools, NGO volunteer orgs, and in HR departments at most medium to large scale workplaces. We would not be off base to say that feminist gatekeeping now regulates much of the planet, from top to bottom. They are everywhere.

But of course when questioned about holding such positions of power, feminists are quick to remind complainants that they still work for the "oppressed" sex and are thus justified in using positions of power to correct global imbalances. Ironically feminists consider power per se bad, a judgment rendering any admission of their own institutional power regulated by a strict taboo – for such an admission is akin to a nun who undertook vows of chastity, and being faced with admitting she is now in a sexual relationship. The authors tell:

> "The first and most persistent form of resistance we have encountered is based on an idea that governance is per se bad, often expressed as an understanding that our describing governance feminism is identical with denouncing it. We do not think it is a gotcha to say that feminism rules."

The lead author Janet Halley admits elsewhere to being an occasional feminist – in other words a feminist if/when the need arises. Nevertheless her adoption of utopic feminist narratives is apparent throughout the pages, as for example when she characterizes feminism, and more specifically Governance Feminism as an "emancipatory project":

> "Feminism is by aspiration an emancipatory project, and GF is one kind of feminists' effort to discover pathways to human emancipation. In the process, GFeminists have been, in some cases, highly successful in changing laws, institutions, and practices, very often remarkably for the better. Just scan the canonical first-wave manifesto for change, the 1848 Seneca Falls Declaration of Sentiments,[4] for once-impossible, now well-established changes in the legal status of U.S. women: the right to vote; the rights of married women to form contracts, to sue and be sued, to acquire and manage separate property, to select their place of residence, to be criminally and civilly responsible for their own actions, to seek a divorce and to seek child custody on formally equal footing with husbands and fathers, and other powers formerly denied to them by coverture; to formally equal access to paid employment; to formally equal access to "wealth and distinction"[5] and to the professions; and to access to education.

These are all basic elements of a liberal feminist agenda for women. Women have devoted entire lifetimes to achieving them. None of them came easily. They are not complete emancipation, surely. But compared with lack of all franchise, coverture, and categorical exclusion from the public sphere and all but the most grinding and ill-paid work, they are immense achievements attributable almost entirely to GFeminist efforts. One reason to describe GF is to be clear about its immense emancipatory achievements."

I can hear the reader's objections now, that Halley's overview of three waves of feminism as 'emancipatory' is a laughable gloss over the violence, censorship and tyranny perpetrated throughout that history. No doubt Halley is here giving a mandatory nod to the narratives of her more powerful "sisters" in order to avoid a backlash.

Framing feminist aspirations as emancipatory, and not as an urge-to-power by ruthless gender-ideologues, softens the tyrannical use of power, painting instead a soothing pastel picture. Said more directly, feminist use of power has to most observers been far more tyrannical and destructive than this glowing characterization reveals. With that in mind the authors might equally have characterized Governance Feminism as unadulterated power-seeking (ultimately for women) and been more on point.

To be fair the authors do go on to tackle some of the excesses of Governance Feminism after their apparently mandatory hand kissing of feminist theorists, and this deeper critique is where the true value of this book lies. The authors admit that many feminist visions of "emancipation" have been left at the station when various governance trains took off, confirming that the '"selective engagement" of feminist ideas into governmental power has left some diamonds in the dust.'

Further, they state;

"In our view it has also done some damage: some governance feminist projects strike us as terrible mistakes; others have unintended consequences that are or should be contested within feminist political life. As some Governance Feminist projects become part of established governance, we find ourselves worrying about them more, or differently, than we did when they were unorthodox, "outsider" ideas. We are, therefore, inviting a robust discussion within feminism and between feminism and its emancipatory allies about which elements are emancipatory and which may, after all, be *mistakes*." [italics mine]

The authors go on to critique a number of these 'mistakes,' while remaining at times uncritical about assumed feminist successes. As touched on above, Governance Feminists also go to great lengths to hide their grasp on power, while taking every opportunity to exaggerate and demonize male uses of power:

"Gender mainstreaming has located feminists in many organizations, from the UN to college administrations, almost always as bureaucrats. Here they wield not judicial power, not the sword of punishment, but the more fine-grained power of administration. Gender mainstreaming, which aims to universalize feminist ideas in governance and convert every governmental entity into a branch of Governance Feminism, paradoxically produces gender specialists."

For most readers this quote encapsulates the danger of feminist power. Feminist ideologues have been inserted into every institution around the globe as gatekeepers dictating who does/doesn't get employed, get assisted, financed, approved, credentialed, included, heard and so on. It can even descend to who gets food aid, who gets to rent a house in a scarce rental market, or who gets a job as a cleaner.

As an example, Jordan Peterson recently talked about HR departments at workplaces serving as foci for the feminist social manipulations. This development is insidious because the practice is hidden in supposedly menial bureaucratic positions, ones that just happen to wield pivotal power over the work-lives of citizens and the associated family outcomes – not to mention the outcome of amplifying gendered expectations and conventions that inevitably get instituted culture-wide through this process of rewarding or punishing via biased bureaucratic decisions. With this in mind it's no exaggeration to call feminists *social engineers* who have succeeded in many of their aims.

Some years ago I read a paper on the topic of "administrative discretion" which refers to the flexible exercising of decision-making allowed to public administrators. The discretionary opportunity is made available by the wiggle-room in the bureaucrat's code of practice, and she or he uses that to deliver preferred – and often unfair – outcomes. The use of administrative discretion typifies the modus operandi of Governance Feminism, which is utilized to implement a radical feminist ideological agenda through all levels of society. Feminism-inspired women are increasingly dominating HR roles, and as revealed by teacher-preferencing biases in elementary schools they are exploiting administrative discretion to favor females over males.

Janet Halley lays much of the blame for the failures of Governance Feminism at the feet of two forms of feminism that form an operational alliance: Power Feminism (PF) and Cultural Feminism (CF). The book provides a useful overview of both, stating that they have formed an unholy alliance that came to dominate the internal battle for supremacy between different 'feminisms.' Power and cultural feminism meld into each other or appear side by side, writes Halley, and together they are frequently dubbed Dominance Feminism. She adds that Dominance Feminism finds male domination in two distinct forms: in the false superiority of male values and male culture, and in the domination of all things Female by all things Male:

> "American dominance feminism is a top-down, bottom-up model of M/F relations: there are perpetrators (men) and victims (women); people with an individualist ethic (men) and people with an ethic of care (women); people feminists advocate for (women) and people they accuse (men). This model of right and wrong is highly assimilable to criminal law and tort law frameworks. Thus the very visible elements of Governance Feminism that use the penal powers of the state to "end" sexual violence in all its forms are saturated with dominance feminist ideas. Especially where power feminism makes its influence felt, it makes sexuality the core of the problem: dominance feminist thinking places

sexual wrongs front and center, and assimilates other seemingly nonsexual wrongs to sexual ones.

This is, we think, a manifestly narrow, crabbed, and even paranoid view of the gender order in the United States, and it is hospitable to quite ethnocentric, neocolonial construals of the gender order prevailing in the global South. It is remarkably indifferent to distributional consequences. Why does it play such a large role in Governance Feminism today?"

In Chapter 3. Halley discusses Governance Feminists' need to reflect on generating, owning, and critiquing their own governance power, which as mentioned above is hamstrung by feminism's denouncement of power structures combined with its own denials about both possessing and wielding real power.

When the authors first encouraged the sustained study of Governance Feminism in 2006, some feminists told them that "they simply did not understand how marginal and fragile feminist gains in state and near-state power really were… If some feminist ideas and interests had managed to find their way into law, these were crumbs from the table, compromises with patriarchy on patriarchy's terms not worthy of the name "feminist," tiny fragments of the full feminist agenda, which was not merely to ride along on the back of power but to transform it."

Such a response is breathtaking in its denial, and I would add predictable, leading the authors to assert that not only do feminists hold such world-changing power, they need also to ethically critique their use of it:

"We think such acts of public critique are absolutely essential now that feminists and feminist ideas are so firmly embedded in legal institutions and legal power.[25] But they can be costly: insider-insiders often feel compelled to attack any feminist who does it, at the very least by depriving her of her insider credentials and her insider job and at the very most by marshaling major institutional resources to discredit her and her ideas, defund her projects, and leave her constituents out in the cold."

In the final chapter Halley implores Governance Feminists to develop an ethic of responsibility; to both admit to the power they preside over, assess its impact both negative and positive, and own the outcome. This lofty appeal is frankly laughable when considering the ideological agendas and unethical practices that Dominance Feminists are known for. Asking them to take a more ethical approach is as likely of success as asking Mao Zedong to develop an ethic of individual liberty and a policy of free-market capitalism.

Antifeminists around the world have a very different suggestion to that of going hat in hand imploring Dominance Feminists to show more ethical and considerate behavior. Their alternative is to shine a harsh light on the moral corruption of feminist ideologues, and work to neutralize their destructive programs via effective counter-activism. The antifeminist counter-movement is in full career and I'm certain that Governance Feminists around the world are already feeling the heat. Halley's book contributes to that insurgency move, perhaps unwittingly, by demonstrating just how much power these ideologues have been wielding. The book is therefore useful in that it speaks the unspeakable... the cat is finally out of the bag.

The authors conclude by mentioning a second volume is in process titled *Governance Feminism: Notes from the Field*, which will provide case studies describing and assessing national, international, and transnational Governance Feminist projects by a range of feminists engaged in building them. No longer operating in the shadows, Governance Feminists are now being scrutinized in broad daylight.... and with that move they will have a lot of explaining to do for their transgressions.

[1] Janet Halley (Author), Prabha Kotiswaran (Author), Rachel Rebouché (Author), Hila Shamir (Author), *Governance Feminism: An Introduction*, by University Of Minnesota Press; (March 13, 2018)

Chivalry feminism

Chivalry and feminism are unrelated, for feminists eschew chivalry as belittling to women, don't they? Well, yes and no.

Over a century ago Ernest B. Bax noticed that feminist rhetoric plays it both ways – i.e., feminists renounce chivalry as demeaning and even victimizing to women on the one hand, and on the other take it up as something to be solicited from every layer of government, business and wider society via overtures about women's vulnerability. As most feminists continue to demonstrate to the very hour, chivalry-seeking remains a core part of the business model - so much so that without it feminism would not be able to exist in its current form.

This comes perhaps as a shock to those among us who would do away with feminism in order to return to a 'traditional' model of sexual relations only to discover that the traditional woman is eerily similar to the new woman in that she too exploits and indeed *expects* male chivalry in similar ways.

Bax describes first-wave feminists as advocating male chivalry for the benefit of women. His assessment in the following quotes underscores how "chivalry feminists," as he called them, and the masses of women influenced by their message, have tended to be duplicitous about their ultimate reliance on chivalry.

Ernest B. Bax on 'Chivalry Feminism'

"I decline to bow down before a sexual principle, or to admit the justice of granting privileges on the basis of a sex-sentiment. What I contended and still contend is that the bulk of the advocates of woman's rights are simply working, not for equality, but for female ascendency. It is all very well to say they repudiate chivalry. They are ready enough to invoke it politically when they want to get a law passed in their favour – while socially, to my certain knowledge, many of them claim it as a right every whit as much as ordinary women.[1]

"Notwithstanding the state of law, public opinion, and custom, the "shrieking sisterhood," and their male lackeys continue to invoke male "chivalry" in defence of every usurpation or act of injustice perpetrated in the interest of female domination… In the early middle ages, when strength of arm was commonly called into requisition for defence, "chivalry" had a meaning; in the nineteenth century it has none, and is merely an excuse for the privileges and domination of the female sex. In fact, if "chivalry" means taking the side of the weaker, it would be shown more often to-day, in championing the cause of the man against the woman, than that of the woman against the man. Hegel said that every typical character appeared twice in history – once as tragedy and once as farce. If we apply this to the chivalric type, and take King Arthur or Sir Launcelot (regarded for the nonce as historical personages) as the embodiment of the former we may certainly find the latter in the person of the great cheap-jack of London journalism, and exponent of the sorrows of husband-hunting wenches. The drop is certainly great from the hero of the "City of Legions" to the "Northumbrian boy."

[…]

In this great step toward *real* as opposed to *sham* equality between the sexes [we require] the repudiation by women themselves of the anachronistic notion of "Chivalry," as being due to them from men. If we are to have equality and fellowship, let it be equality and fellowship, and not a hollow fraud masquerading under the name.[2]

Let women have the franchise by all means, provided two things, first of all: provided you can get rid of their present practical immunity from the operation of the criminal law for all offences committed against men and of the gallantry and shoddy chivalry that now hedges a woman in all relations of life.[3]

"THE justification for the whole movement of Modern Feminism in one of its main practical aspects – namely, the placing of the female sex in the position of privilege, advantage and immunity – is concentrated in the current conception of "chivalry." It behoves us, therefore, to devote some consideration to the meaning and implication of this notion. Now this word chivalry is the *dernier ressort* of those at a loss for a justification of the modern privileging of women.[4]

"It is plain then that chivalry as understood in the present day really spells sex privilege and sex favouritism pure and simple, and that any attempts to define the term on a larger basis, or to give it a colourable rationality founded on fact, are simply subterfuges, conscious or unconscious, on the part of those who put them forward.[4]

"Every outrageous pretension of Sentimental Feminism can be justified by the appeal to chivalry, which amounts (to use the German expression) to an appeal from Pontius to Pilate. This Sentimental Feminism commonly called chivalry is sometimes impudently dubbed by its votaries, "manliness." It will presumably continue in its practical effects until a sufficient minority of sensible men will have the moral courage to beard a Feminist public opinion and shed a little of this sort of "manliness."[4]

"Such is "chivalry" as understood to-day – the deprivation, the robbery from men of the most elementary personal rights in order to endow women with privileges at the expense of men.[4]

But these considerations afford only one more illustration of the utter irrationality of the whole movement of Sentimental Feminism identified with the notion of "chivalry." For the rest, we may find illustrations of this galore. A very flagrant case is that infamous "rule of the sea" which came so much into prominence at the time of the Titanic disaster. According to this preposterous "chivalric" Feminism, in the case of a ship foundering, it is the unwritten law of the seas, not that the passengers shall leave the ship and be rescued in their order as they come, but that the whole female portion shall have the right of being rescued before any man is allowed to leave the ship. Now this abominable piece of sex favouritism, on the face of it, cries aloud in its irrational injustice.[4]

"Chivalry, as understood by Modern Sentimental Feminism, means unlimited licence for women in their relations with men, and unlimited coercion for men in their relations with women. To men all duties and no rights, to women all rights and no duties, is the basic principle underlying Modern Feminism, Suffragism, and the bastard chivalry it is so fond of invoking. The most insistent female shrieker for equality between the sexes among Political Feminists, it is interesting to observe, will, in most cases, on occasion be found an equally insistent advocate of the claims of Sentimental Feminism, based on modern metamorphosed notions of chivalry. It never seems to strike anyone that the muscular weakness of woman has been forged by Modern Feminists into an abominable weapon of tyranny. Under cover of the notion of chivalry, as understood by Modern Feminism, Political and Sentimental Feminists alike would deprive men of the most elementary rights of self-defence against women and would exonerate the latter practically from all punishment for the most dastardly crimes against men. They know they can rely upon the support of the sentimental section of public opinion with some such parrot cry of' "What! Hit a woman!"

Why not, if she molests you?

"Treat a woman in this way!" "Shame!" responds automatically the crowd of Sentimental Feminist idiots, oblivious of the fact that the real shame lies in their endorsement of an iniquitous sex privilege. If the same crowd were prepared to condemn any special form of punishment or mode of treatment as inhumane for both sexes alike, there would, of course, be nothing to be said. But it is not so. The most savage cruelty and vindictive animosity towards men leaves them comparatively cold, at most evoking a mild remonstrance as against the inflated manifestation of sentimental horror and frothy indignation produced by any slight hardship inflicted by way of punishment (let us say) on a female offender."[5]

––––––––––––––

"In the foregoing pages we have endeavoured to trace some of the leading strands of thought going to make up the Modern Feminist Movement. Sentimental Feminism clearly has its roots in sexual feeling, and in the tradition of chivalry, albeit the notion of chivalry has essentially changed in the course of its evolution. For the rest, Sentimental Feminism, with its double character of man-antipathy and woman-sympathy, as we see it to-day, has assumed the character of one of those psychopathic social phenomena which have so often recurred in history. It can only be explained, like the latter, as an hypnotic wave passing over society.[5]

Sources:

[1] *No Misogyny But True Equality* in *To-Day*, October 1887, pp.115-121
[2] Some Heterodox Notes on the Woman Question (1887)
[3] The "Monstrous Regiment" of Womanhood (1907), in *Essays in Socialism New & Old* (1907), pp.108-119.
[4] Chapter-5 'The Chivalry Fake' in *The Fraud of Feminism*, 1913

[5] <u>Chapter-7: 'The Psychology of the Movement'</u> *The Fraud of Feminism*, 1913

The roots of feminism

While it may seem like a topic of modern men's movement, the burning question of whether men should marry, or more to the point, *not* marry, is centuries old. That men are rejecting marriage in increasing numbers today is well documented, however cynicism about the virtues of marriage is nothing new.

In the premodern period there appeared a movement called the *Querelle des Femmes* or quarrel about women, which approximates to the current debate between feminists and antifeminists. The centuries-long *querelle* revolved around discussion of the rights, power and status of women. At its extremes the debate showcased hatred of women on the one hand, and extreme adoration or love of women on the other.

In its broader sense, the *querelle* encompasses all writing in which the relative merits of the sexes are discussed to ultimately draw gynocentric conclusions. If we consider the longevity of this revolution we can say that today's feminism is the tail end of a longer advocacy machine for women.

The timeframe of the *querelle* begins in the twelfth century, and after 800 years of debate finds itself perpetuated in the feminist-driven reiterations of today (though some authors claim, unconvincingly, that the *querelle* came to an end in the 1700s).

The following excerpt from a paper discussing the *querelle*, by historian Joan Kelly, is instructive. It was written with a feminist focus, thus leaving out all but the most superficial characterization of the male experience of gender relations. Nevertheless it provides much important history about the longer gender debate and how it underpinned the growth of modern feminism:

> We generally think of feminism, and certainly of feminist theory, as taking rise in the nineteenth and twentieth centuries. Most histories of the Anglo-American women's movement acknowledge feminist "forerunners" in individual figures such as Anne Hutchinson, and in women inspired by the English and French revolutions, but only with the women's rights conference at Seneca Falls in 1848 do they recognize the beginnings of a continuously developing body of feminist thought. Histories of French feminism claim a longer past.
>
> They tend to identify Christine de Pisan (1364-1430?) as the first to hold modern feminist views and then to survey other early figures who followed her in expressing prowoman ideas up until the time of the French Revolution. New work is now appearing that will give us a fuller sense of the richness, coherence, and continuity of early feminist thought, and I hope this paper contributes to that end. What I hope to demonstrate is that there was a 400-year-old tradition of women thinking about women and sexual politics in European society *before* the French Revolution.

Feminist theorizing arose in the fifteenth century, in intimate association with and in reaction to the new secular culture of the modern European state. It emerged as the voice of literate women who felt themselves and all women maligned and newly oppressed by that culture, but who were empowered by it at the same time to speak out in their defense. Christine de Pisan was the first such feminist thinker, and the four-century-long debate that she sparked, known as the *querelle des femmes*, became the vehicle through which most early feminist thinking evolved.

The early feminists did not use the term "feminist," of course. If they had applied any name to themselves, it would have been something like defenders or advocates of women, but it is fair to call this long line of prowomen writers that runs from Christine de Pisan to Mary Wollstonecraft by the name we use for their nineteenth- and twentieth-century descendants. Latter-day feminism, for all its additional richness, still incorporates the basic positions the feminists of the *querelle* were the first to take.[1]

Kelly's paper is worth reading in full, but as mentioned above the author leaves out a substantial exploration of the male experience within the *querelle*. For the record I would also place the beginnings of the Querelle back further than the usual dates ascribed to it, and least to the writing of *The Romance Of The Rose* and earlier to the treatise *The Art of Courtly Love* which both discuss themes of the emergent *querelle*, and both generated lively social debate on women's status and gendered issues.

In essence the *querelle* consisted of a perpetual social movement that exploited the *damsel in distress* trope to call for more chivalry and more courtly love, which ultimately afforded women more power.

The three elements of gynocentrism first born in medieval Europe – damseling, chivalry and courtly love – continue to act as the basis of modern feminism. Indeed feminism today is little more, and little less, than a perpetuation of this medieval triad, giving feminism its internal drive even as feminists disavow these essentials with rhetorical obfuscations.

With this charge in mind let's revisit the holy trinity above with a focus on behaviors central to modern feminism.

Damseling as "victim feminism"

Most observers today, including feminist observers like Christina Hoff-Sommers, Camille Paglia, Rene Denfeld, Katie Roiphe and others agree that feminism comes close, if not all the way, to being a cult of victimhood.

The phenomenon has variously been referred to as grievance feminism, victim feminism, safe space feminism, and even fainting-couch feminism – with Christina Hoff-Sommers portraying its mythos as "a battle between fragile maidens and evil predators." [2]

Feminist icon Naomi Wolf tells that victim feminism evolved out of "old habits of ladylike behavior that were cloaked in the guise of radicalism," [3] and laments that a substantial segment of modern feminism is devoted to its cause.

Denfeld writes that current feminists "promote a new status for women: that of the victim," and adds:

> "This is victim mythology. From rape redefinitions to feminist theory on the "patriarchy," victimization has become the subtext of the movement, the moral to be found in every feminist story. Together these stories form a feminist mythology in which a singular female subject is created: woman as a helpless, violated, and oppressed victim. Victim mythology says that men will always be predators and women will always be their prey. It is a small place to live, a place that tells women that there is really no way out.

> "Like other mythologies, victim mythology reduces the complexity of human interaction to grossly oversimplified mythical tales, a one-note song, where the message of the story becomes so important that fiction not only triumphs over fact but the realities of women's experiences are dismissed and derided when they conflict with the accepted female image.[4]

While Denfeld does a good job of describing feminism's victim mentality, she labors under a myth of her own by characterizing it as a "new" fetish among feminists.

Anyone reading through the history of feminist literature can see it appealed to by literally every feminist writer. Even a century ago Ernest Belfort Bax was able to say that feminists "do their best to bluff their dupes by posing as the victims of a non-existent male oppression."[5]

> Feminists well know that the most grotesquely far-fetched cry about the injustice of man to woman will meet with a ready ear. They well know that they get here fond and foolish man on his soft side. Looking at the matter impartially, it is quite evident that man's treatment of woman is the least vulnerable point in his moral record. Woman, as such, he has always treated with comparative generosity. But it is, of course, to the interests of the abettors of female domination to pretend the contrary. Accordingly everything has been done to excite prejudice in favour of woman as the innocent and guileless *victim* of man's tyranny, and the maudlin Feminist sentiment of the "brute" man has been carefully exploited to this end.[6]

In all of these accounts the behavior being described is *damseling*, a practice feminists have been at the forefront of preserving from the medieval canon. Evoked in conjunction with claims of male brutality, rapiness, depravity and insensitivity, the ultimate purpose of damseling is to draw chivalric responses from men, a routine Wolf makes clear in her remark that "victim feminism casts women as sexually pure and mystically nurturing, and stresses the evil done to these 'good' women as a way to petition for their rights." [7]

A famous example of feminist damseling, both literal and figurative, is Anita Sarkeesian. Sarkeesian is known for raising concerns that video-games are misogynistic – like most everything else found in the feminist worldview. Her primary concern was that female game characters are often portrayed as damsels-in-distress saved by male heroes, which promotes, she says, sexual objectification and a range of other problems. To address that issue in video games she moved to launch a study project to raise awareness.

Sarkeesian established a fundraiser for $6,000.00 for her project, but after receiving some initial trolling by trolls on social media she damseled herself to potential donors by saying she was under grave threat, swooning with such finesse that she was showered with 158K in donations from fellow feminists and white knights. Over a thousand people donated after hearing of her "plight."

With that financial success, Sarkeesian subsequently replayed the scenario over and again particularly in the context of further fundraising efforts and public speaking; swooning about online attacks directed against her or over female gamers enduring abject sexism, female video-game characters being cast in degrading and/or humiliating roles, and about young impressionable girls being robbed of agency after being subjected to the damsel trope in games.

Sarkeesian's case is particularly poignant because, from the many subjects she could have highlighted to damsel herself for attention, she chose to damsel herself over the very existence of damsels. This demonstrates that even when disavowing the medieval pageant of damsels in distress, feminists continue to enact it even while obfuscating their complicity in the tradition.

Feminism would have died out long ago if it were not for the power of this ancient ruse, and while damseling continues to draw rewards from a public primed to cater to it, the planet will increasingly come to resemble a tower full of imprisoned, vulnerable Disney Princesses.

Chivalry – from husband Sam to Uncle Sam

Equity feminist Christina Hoff-Sommers states that men need to be civilized with chivalric manners, a belief outlined in an interview with Emily Esfahani Smith, where she said, "Chivalry is grounded in a fundamental reality that defines the relationship between the sexes," and adding a warning, "If women give up on chivalry, it will be gone." [8]

While feminists like Hoff-Sommers admit their reliance on a sexist version of chivalry, others are less candid about it, going even so far as pretending they don't need chivalry despite their demonstrable appeal to it in most of their activism. Many observers however can see through the anti-chivalry posturing.

Feminism draws its power from chivalric support, but instead of soliciting it from men in the traditional, interpersonal manner it has learned how to get it solely from the government – holding the government to ransom ever since the suffragettes damseled the vote for women. Since that time politicians have only been too willing to furnish demands by feminists in exchange for voting the candidate into power and allowing him to retain office –

and conversely politicians who fail to uphold the chivalric contract are promptly voted out.

The results of this compact are obvious to anyone who looks at political decisions with impartiality.

Instead of men giving up seats in buses, government now provides seats in legislative assemblies and boardrooms via quotas. Instead of men opening car doors for women, government opens doors into universities and workforces via affirmative action. Instead of men being the sole protectors of women from violence, government now protects them with an army of police specially trained to service women's accusations (over and above more serious crimes). Instead of men providing living expenses, governments now provide it as social welfare and compensation for the wage-gap. Government as substitute husband.

The appeal to chivalry is not confined to government institutions alone. The appeal also goes out to sporting clubs, business owners, CEOs and private institutions who respond to the damsel's call with women-only busses, women-only safe spaces, pink car parking spaces with extra lighting and security with male escorts and chaperones, or with feminist adverts at sports venues, sportsmen wearing pink to raise money for all manner of feminist projects, and that on top of monies already heaped at their feet by politicians eager to please.

This is not a recent development; it can be witnessed in mirror image as far back as a century ago. Back then, Bax was able to tie feminism so definitively with the act of chivalry-seeking that he actually labeled the women's liberation movement "chivalry feminism." Moreover, Bax saw through the superficial disavowals;

> "The justification for the whole movement of Modern Feminism in one of its main practical aspects – namely, the placing of the female sex in the position of privilege, advantage and immunity – is concentrated in the current conception of "chivalry."

> It is plain then that chivalry as understood in the present day really spells sex privilege and sex favouritism pure and simple, and that any attempts to define the term on a larger basis, or to give it a colourable rationality founded on fact, are simply subterfuges, conscious or unconscious, on the part of those who put them forward...

> Such is "chivalry" as understood to-day – the deprivation, the robbery from men of the most elementary personal rights in order to endow women with privileges at the expense of men.[9]

Chivalry feminism today, same as it ever was, relying on men's generosity to perpetuate its creed of power.

Courtly love as 'Respectful Relationships'

The phrase 'Respectful Relationships' is shorthand for a range of conventions promoted by feminists to govern interactions between men and women, particularly in the context of romantic interactions. The conventions detail acceptable speech and actions in the contexts of socializing, friendship, flirting and sex, emphasizing a man's duty to respect women's emotional comfort, self-esteem, and dignity.

Portrayed overtly as a method of reducing men's abusiveness, the program maintains that even men and boys who do *not* display abusive behaviors should be enculturated in its protocols as a prophylactic, and concomitantly to afford dignity and self-esteem to women. This is where the respectful relationships program moves past the overt goal of reducing violence and into the covert goal of maintaining and increasing the power of women.

As we begin to look at the detail of Respectful Relationship we could almost mistake it for Andreas Capellanus' work *The Art of Courtly Love* where the medieval rules of romance were codified in meticulous prescriptions for male deference, homage, and courtesy toward women. Considering this parallel, the feminist movement appears to have provided a new language for a very old set of sexual customs, essentially reiterating that which has been with us all along.

A central to the art of courtly love was the expectation that men practice *love service* toward women based on a model of vassals or serfs in relation to a feudal lord. That relationship model of serf-to-Lord was adopted wholesale to regulate love relationships whereby women were literally approached as the lord (*midons*) in each male-female encounter. As Medievalist Sandra Alfonsi explains;

> Scholars soon saw striking parallels between
> feudalistic practices and certain tenets of Courtly

Love. The comparisons lie in certain resemblances shared by vassalage and the courtly "love service." Fundamental to both was the concept of obedience. As a vassal, the liegeman swore obedience to his lord. As a courtly lover, the poet chose a lady to whom he was required to swear obedience. Humility and obedience were two concepts familiar to medieval man, active components of his Weltanschauung...

The entire concept of love-service was patterned after the vassal's oath to serve his lord with loyalty, tenacity, and courage. These same virtues were demanded of the poet. Like the liegeman vis-a-vis his sovereign, the poet approached his lady with fear and respect. Submitted to her, obedient to her will, he awaited a fief or honor as did the vassal. His compensation took many forms: the pleasure of his lady's company in her chamber or in the garden; an avowal of her love; a secret meeting; a kiss or even le surplus, complete unity. Like the lord, the woman who was venerated and served was expected to reward her faithful and humble servant.[10]

The idea behind love service was that men should demonstrate the quality of their commitment to women; was it merely lust or obedient and sacrificial love? If the woman decided it was "love" then she might decide to engage more intimately with him, as Joseph Campbell explains:

"The woman is looking for authenticity in a relationship, so she delays *merci* until she is

guaranteed that this man who is proposing himself
to her is one of a gentle heart… And, the women
were in control, that's all there is to it. The man is
the one who is advancing, the one performing the
acts of guarding bridges, or whatever bit of
foolishness she puts on him, but, she's in control.
And her problem is to live in a relationship that is
authentic of love, and the only way she can do it
is by testing the one who offers himself. She isn't
offering herself, he's offering himself. But, she's
in control of what happens then with step two.[11]

"The technical term for a woman's granting of
herself was *merci*; the woman grants her merci.
Now, that might consist in her permission for the
man to kiss her on the back of the neck once
every Whitsuntide, you know, something like that
– or it may be a full giving in love. That would
depend upon her estimation of the character of the
candidate. The essential idea was to test this man
to make sure that he would suffer things for love,
and that this was not just lust.

The tests that were given then by women
involved, for example, sending a chap out to
guard a bridge. The traffic in the Middle Ages
was somewhat encumbered by these youths
guarding bridges. But also the tests included
going into battle. A woman who was too ruthless
in asking her lover to risk a real death before she
would acquiesce in anything was considered
sauvage or "savage". Also, the woman who gave
herself without the testing was "savage". There

was a very nice psychological estimation game going on here.[12]

Today that psychological estimation game (as Campbell puts it) might involve asking consent to sit with a woman, appealing politely for a date, waiting patiently for her to call or sweep right, keeping his knees together to avoid manspreading, or asking for permission to speak in order to prove he is not talking over her or mansplaining. Such demonstrations show the feminist woman that he has a gentle heart, and that he is willing to suffer things for love.

That psychological testing also encompasses public activities which demonstrate a man's commitment to serving womankind as a whole. Examples would be a man walking a mile in her shoes, or joining White Ribbon Campaigns that require men, as was required of the medieval knights, to pledge oaths to "Never to condone, or remain silent about violence towards women and girls" and especially to *intervene* when learning of any male behaving offensively toward a woman.

Today's White Ribbon "oath" bears a striking resemblance to the 14th century enterprise of the Green Shield with the White Lady (*Emprise de l'Escu vert à la Dame Blanche*) in which men committed themselves for the duration of five years to serving women. Inspired by the ideal of courtly love, the stated purpose of the order was to guard and defend the honor, estate, goods, reputation, fame and praise of all ladies. It was an undertaking that earned the praise of protofeminist Christine de Pizan. The continuity of chivalry and courtly love from the medieval knightly oath to the modern feminist-inspired oath is remarkable in its consistency.

In line with most women who expect men to follow medieval rules of love concerning male courtesy, the feminist movement is geared toward enforcing the same goal. Feminism however *postures* itself as disavowing that goal even while they are at the forefront of institutionalizing it in our families, our schools, our political structures and laws.

Each of the psychological tests mentioned above are evidence of a *love service* called for by feminist activists. Or worded differently, they are sanctified methods by which men are called to demonstrate obedience and a 'gentle heart' in contrast to the brutality, rapiness and exploitativeness of the savage heart; the default feminist conception of men.

I will close here with the words of an academic feminist, one not so coy about identifying courtly love with the project of feminism. Elizabeth Reid Boyd of the School of Psychology and Social Science at Edith Cowan University, and Director of the Centre for Research for Women in Western Australia with more than a decade as a feminist researcher and teacher of women's studies tells:

> In this article I muse upon arguments that romance is a form of feminism. Going back to its history in the Middle Ages and its invention by noblewomen who created the notion of courtly love, examining its contemporary popular explosion and the concurrent rise of popular

romance studies in the academy that has emerged in the wake of women's studies, and positing an empowering female future for the genre, I propose that reading and writing romantic fiction is not only personal escapism, but also political activism.

Romance has a feminist past that belies its ostensible frivolity. Romance, as most true romantics know, began in medieval times. The word originally referred to the language romanz, linked to the French, Italian and Spanish languages in which love stories, songs and ballads were written. Stories, poems and songs written in this language were called romances to separate them from more serious literature – a distinction we still have today. Romances were popular and fashionable. Love songs and stories, like those of Lancelot and Guinevere, Tristan and Isolde, were soon on the lips of troubadours and minstrels all over Europe. Romance spread rapidly. It has been called the first form of feminism (Putnam 1970).[13]

Reid Boyd finishes her paper by waxing poetic about the many joys of romantic love, and of its increasing popularity in academe.

Same as it ever was, the project of modern feminism can be summarized as championing victimhood (damseling), soliciting favors from men and governments (chivalry), and promoting "respectful" relationships by men-toward-women (courtly love).

References:

[1] Joan Kelly, *Early Feminist Theory and the "Querelle des Femmes", 1400-1789*

[2] Christina Hoff-Sommers, *How fainting couch feminism threatens freedom*, American Enterprise Institute 2015

[3] Naomi Wolf, *Fire With Fire: New Female Power*, 1993

[4] Rene Denfeld, *The New Victorians: A Young Woman's Challenge to the Old Feminist Order*, 1995

[5] Ernest B. Bax, *Feminism and Female Suffrage*, 1910

[6] Ernest B. Bax, *Mr. Belfort Bax Replies to his Feminist Critics*, 1908

[7] Naomi Wolf, *Fire With Fire: New Female Power*, 1993

[8] Emily Esfahani Smith, *Let's Give Chivalry Another Chance,* The Atlantic, Dec 10 2012

[9] Ernest B. Bax, Chapter-5 'The Chivalry Fake' in *The Fraud of Feminism*, 1913

[10] Sandra Alfonsi, *Masculine Submission in Troubadour Lyric*, 1986

[11] Joseph Campbell, *Parzival, the Graal, and Grail Legends*, talk at the Ojai Foundation, 1987

[12] Joseph Campbell, *The Power of Myth*, interview with Bill Moyers, 1988

[13] Elizabeth Reid Boyd, *Romancing Feminism: From Women's Studies to Women's Fiction*, 2014

A collective nagathon

I recently mentioned to a friend that feminist verbiage amounts to little more than organized female nagging — the endless attempt to shame & guilt men into serving women. Is it any wonder that feminist street placards emphasise "having a voice," "women speaking up," "not being silenced," and "speaking out"? These phrases are nothing more than euphemisms for the ear piercing, fingernails-on-blackboard nagging that women have never gone without. Sadly, the days of being able to deal with nagging by use the following device are long gone:

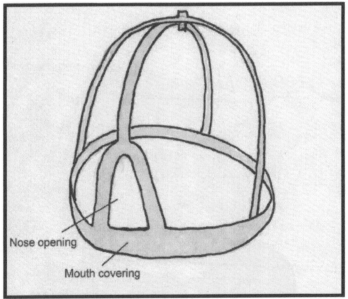

Scold's bridle: historical mouth-covering device used to discipline the nagging women [Author's drawing]

So universal is the archetype of the nagging woman that I visited Amazon in the certainty that someone would have written a book titled "The History Of Female Nagging," but to my surprise found there was none.

I guess its like other universals such as 'everyone has a buttocks,' – so blatantly obvious that no book is necessary. That said, I still wanted to dig deeper into the topic and so decided to check an online etymology dictionary, which reads as follows:

> **nag (v.)**
> 1828, intransitive, "find fault constantly;" by 1840, intransitive, "annoy by continued scolding, pester with petty complaints," originally a dialectal word meaning "to gnaw" (1825, Halliwell), probably ultimately from a Scandinavian source (compare Old Norse *gnaga* "to complain," literally "to bite, gnaw," dialectal Swedish and Norwegian *nagga* "to gnaw"), from Proto-Germanic *gnagan*, related to Old English *gnagan* "to gnaw" (see gnaw). As a noun, 1894, "act of nagging;" by 1925, "person who nags." Related: *Nagged; nagger; nagging.*[1]

What struck me here was the association of nagging with acts of biting and gnawing, which is exactly what feels like is happening to your soul when being nagged, as any man or child will confirm. In this respect it reminds of the mythical eagle gnawing at the liver of Prometheus, only to have it happen again the very next day in an endless round of torture.

Considering the longevity and ubiquity of female nagging, and considering also that gynocentrism and feminism are collective nagathons, I think the future looks bleak in terms of a breakthrough for men. Our modern world has successfully institutionalized nagging at the highest levels – from the United Nations to national governments, and all the way down to schools.

This leads to the disturbing definition of feminism as "Institutionalized female nagging."

Let the naggers chew on that definition for a while.

Perhaps we can put a positive spin on it and say that the drip, drip, drip of female nagging, from bassinet to coffin, has a *toughening* effect on men, bringing out the best of stoic resistance and emotional control that men are famed for. At least when its not driving men to die early, or to suicide at four times the rate of women.

Having got the gist of what I already knew about nagging, I searched the internet a bit further and noticed the following blog article, which is relegated to Creative Commons. It digs a bit deeper into the topic, so I repost the following excerpts for your interest:

A brief history of nagging

The nagging wife is the universal villain of married life. From the earliest pages of human history there is perhaps no literature and folk tradition where the character of the nagging wife is not found widely. Along with archetypes of the sacrificing mother, forsaken lover, tragic hero and evil lord, the nagging wife will be found in all societies and cultures at all times in history. Even in today's world, irrespective of the differences of race, wealth, religion, culture, language and social reform, the character of the nagging wife is universal. She keeps popping up in jokes, films, songs, novels and other cultural cultural creations.

Socrates, the famous Greek philosopher, is supposed to have had a nagging wife who drove him to spend his time in the city squares and gymnasia, much to the benefit of philosophy. The figure of the nagging wife finds mention in the Bible, (indirectly) in the Quran, and is a crucial moment in the story of the Ramayana. She is to be found in renassaince Italy, in medieval England, on the expanding border of America's "wild west", in the bedrooms of colonial India and in the sit-coms of post-modern Europe.

What is interesting about this figure of the nagging wife is that it is one of those few characters who transcend history. Like the sacrificing mother, the unrequited lover or the tragic hero, the nagging wife can be found in ancient, slave owning agricultural societies, in prosperous trading medieval ones and in post-industrial wastelands of contemporary West. What is it about the nagging wife which makes this character so universal and transcendental?

***

It is not only the wife who deploys this weapon of the weak. Children use it to excellent effect. In that context (parent – child) it is not generally called nagging but rather 'pestering'. It too emerges from a similar context of powerlessness of children within the family, where the only way for them to get their point across is to 'pester' their parents till they accept defeat. Today, the power of children to pester their parents into taking decisions is an important weapon in the arsenal of advertisers who use "pester-power" to sell everything from groceries to cars.

In the contemporary world, many families have moved out of the context under which nagging by wives exists. Women own property, often they are in positions of power and are effective decision makers. Nagging does not automatically end in these contexts, just like it does not automatically exist in all patriarchal families. Today nagging is not necessarily confined to the patriarchal family and has been, in a sense, freed from the context of the patriarchal family under which it originated and survived. It has become a cultural archetype which women (and men) absorb into their personalities in the process of socialisation. Where it exists outside the immediate context of the patriarchal family, it exists only as a weapon of offence and not as a survival skill of the weak wife and it "forges its own chains" for those who deploy it in inter-personal relations. The question arises, are we courageous enough to surrender this weapon? [2]

References:

[1] Nag, in *Online Etymology Dictionary*.
[2] Aniket Alam, *A brief history of nagging*, Creative Commons(2008)

The other beauty myth

In 1991 feminist Naomi Wolf wrote *The Beauty Myth*
where she claimed that powerless women are oppressed
by cultural pressure to be beautiful. What she failed to
tell us is where this habit originated, and how it is
essentially used to gain power over the male sex.

In human beings, various compulsions and desires come
into conflict with one another, each jostling for
momentary supremacy where one imperative will usurp
the claims of another. That game has reached a
problematical impasse during the last 800 years because,
during that relatively short time span, human culture has
thrown its weight into developing, intensifying and
enforcing sexual gamesmanship to the degree that our
sexual compulsions appear pumped up on steroids and
taken to extremes never before seen in human society
(myths about widespread Roman orgies notwithstanding).
The obsession with female beauty forms a significant part
of the problem, and the feminist movement has been no
less complicit in celebrating it, even as they choose to
play a double-hand.

If we lived back in Ancient Greece, Rome or anywhere
else we would view sexual intercourse as little more than
a bodily function akin to eating, shitting and sleeping – a
basic bodily function without the hype. After the Middle
Ages, however, it developed into a commodity to pimp
and trade, and the new cult of sexualized romance that
arose from it resulted in a frustration of our more basic
attachment needs – a frustration aided and abetted by

social institutions placing sexual manipulation at the center of human interaction. This development entrenched a new belief that beauty was the native possession of women, and only women, and conversely that the desire to possess beauty was the lot of males alone, thus creating a division between the sexes that remains in place today.

Compare this division with the beliefs of older cultures – India, Rome, Greece etc – and we see a stark contrast, with classical cultures equally apportioning beauty to males and sexual desire to females. In Ancient Greece for example males used to grow their hair long and comb it adoringly, rub olive oil on their skin and pay devoted attention to attire -the colors of the toga, the materials it was woven from, the way it was draped on the body- and there is perhaps no modern culture on earth where male beauty is more marvelously celebrated in the arts than it was in Greece.

Another example comes from the Biblical Song of Solomon, in which the appreciation of beauty and associated longing flows both ways between the man and women, whereas in romantic love beauty is ascribed only to the female, and desire only to the male – the roles are radically split. Moreover, in the Song of Songs there is no hint of the gynocentric arrangement; no appearance of man as a vassal towards women who are both Lord and deity. For the lovers in Song of Songs there already exists a God and so there is no worshipping of the woman as a quasi divinity who can redeem the man's pathetic existence – as in "romantic" love.

According to Robert Solomon, romantic love required a dramatic change in the self-conception of women. He recounts;

> They too were freed from an identity that depended wholly on their social roles, that is, their blood and legal ties with men, as daughters, wives and mothers. It is in this period in Christian history that *looks* become of primary importance, that being beautiful now counts for possibly everything, not just an attractive feature in a daughter or wife (which probably counted very little anyway) but as itself a mark of character, style, personality. Good grooming, as opposed to propriety, came to define the individual woman, and her worth, no longer dependent on the social roles and positions of her father, husband or children, now turned on her looks. The premium was placed on youth and beauty, and though some women even then may have condemned this emphasis as unjust, it at least formed the first breach with a society that, hitherto, had left little room for personal initiative or individual advancement. The prototype of the *Playboy* playmate, we might say, was already established eight hundred years ago, and did not require, as some people have argued recently, Hugh Hefner's slick centerfolds to make youth, beauty and a certain practiced vacuity into a highly esteemed personal virtue. The problem is why we still find it difficult to move *beyond* this without, like some Platonists, distaining beauty altogether – the opposite error.[1]

Modesta Pozzo penned a book in the 1500's entitled *The Worth of Women: their Nobility and Superiority to Men.* The work purportedly records a conversation among seven Venetian noblewomen that explores nearly every aspect of women's experience. One of the topics explored is women's use of cosmetics and clothing to enhance beauty, including mention of hair tinting for which there is twenty-six different recipes. The following is the voice of Cornelia who explains that men's sexual desire of women (and women's control of that process via beauty) is the only reason men can love:

> "Thinking about it straight, what more worthy and what lovelier subject can one find than the beauty, grace and virtues of women?... I'd say that a perfectly composed outer corporeal form is something most worthy of our esteem, for it is this visible outer form that is the first to present itself to our eye and our understanding: we see it and instantly love and desire it, prompted by an instinct embedded in us by nature. "It's not because men love us that they go in for all these displays of love and undying devotion, rather, it's because they desire us. So that in this case love is the offspring, desire the parent, or, in other words, love is the effect and desire the cause. And since taking away the cause means taking away the effect, that means that men love us for just as long as they desire us and once desire, which is the cause of their vain love, has died in them (either because they have got what they wanted or because they have realized that they are not going to be able to get it), the love that is the effect of that cause dies at exactly the same time."[2]

What I find interesting is that since the Middle Ages, as evidenced in Cornelia's words, we have collectively conflated male love with sexual desire as if they are inseparable, and to women's ability to control that male "love" through a skillful cultivation of beauty. One might be forgiven for refusing to believe this is love at all, that it is instead the creation of an intense desire for sexual pleasure due to the appeal of beauty. However observation often reveals that beauty and sex-generated "love" does not lead to compatibility for partners across a broad range of interests, and in fact may occur between people who are, aside from sexual attraction, totally incompatible, with little in common, which is why the relationship often goes so badly when there gaps in the sexual game occur.

This raises the alternative notion of love based on compatibility, on what we might term 'friendship-love' which is not based solely on sexual desire – in fact sexual desire is not even essential to it even if often present. Friendship love is about interests the partners share in common, a meeting of compatible souls and a getting to know each other on a level playing field. However aiming for friendship-love means women are no longer required to pull the strings of sexual desire as is practiced with beauty-based allure, which ultimately frees men and women to meet as equals in power and, with luck, find much in common to sustain a durable relationship.

[1] Robert Solomon, *Love: Emotion, Myth, Metaphor*, 1990 (p.62)

[2] Modesta Pozzo, *The Worth of Women: their Nobility and Superiority to Men*, 2007
[3] Nancy Friday, *The Power of Beauty*, 1997

Harvesting the male gaze

Feminist theory has taught us about the male gaze and the resultant sexualization of the female body that it creates. The standard accusation is that men are scanning their environment for hapless women to perv on, an act that reduces women from otherwise complex human beings to mere sex objects for male sexual pleasure. The following Oxford Reference Dictionary definition represents the usual view of the male gaze, or at least the one widely promoted by feminist analysis of the phenomenon:

Male Gaze

1. A manner of treating women's bodies as objects to be surveyed, which is associated by feminists with hegemonic masculinity, both in everyday social interaction and in relation to their representation in visual media: [see also objectification].

What stands out in all definitions of the gaze is men's agency: men "treat" women's bodies, "survey" women's bodies, and enact "hegemony" over women's bodies. It's a travesty that deprives women of agency according to the feminist film critic credited with first coining "the male gaze."[1]

Is the feminist explanation correct; are women always passive victims of rapey stares, or are they playing their part in eliciting it from men? Might it be – shock, horror

– that women are agent provocateurs in a game they initiate and to a large extent control? Are they "asking for it"? I think most people, at least those not in denial, know the answer to that question is a big yes.

The hours and years spent trying on different clothing, and the rehearsing of postures, or gestures of the hands in front of the mirror (touching her face, placing them on her hips, or lightly above her breasts; or the practicing of facial gestures), and the smiles, pursed lips, head-tilts, hair flicks, and glances of the eyes, all designed to harvest the gaze from unsuspecting male targets.

Could it be that through that highly cultivated repertoire of gestures women possess enormous agency, and males serve as passive targets with little agency other than unprocessed reactivity?

Whatever the case we first need to rid ourselves of the myth that women are victims in this age-old game, to which end I will give a few gaze-harvesting techniques employed by women below, a list that can easily be expanded by adding your own observations of harvesting tricks.

Here are some of the techniques women habitually use to *set a gaze reaction in motion*, each of which involves a woman actively – and sometimes aggressively – placing herself within your sensory range with one of the following:

The Twisty Twirl

The best way to describe this is a gentle swaying or twisting the body from side to side, often with hands clasped at front, to impart a childish exuberance much like little girls do. While this might seem appropriate behavior of a 5 year old girl, the twisty-twirl is not something the gaze harvesting woman ever relinquishes – she employs it to interrupt men's field of vision with sudden movement, a gesture sufficient to gain his attention.

The Blockade

This happens when you are the target of a woman who wants to slow you down and make you absorb her presence. She will stand in the doorway, middle of the footpath, or in the shopping center aisle sometimes aided by a shopping trolley which she leaves strategically placed across the aisle. If done well, this forces an interaction: "Excuse me, I'll just move your trolley so I can get past," to which she replies "Oh, I'm so sorry," while flashing her most attractive features at you – her favorite dress, beautifully shampoo'd hair, or that smile she was famed for in high school.

The Color Assault

The practice of wearing eye-seizing colors is a favorite, with the unmistakable message being YOU WILL LOOK AT ME AND SEE ME! Gone are the soft pastel designs of yesteryear, and in are the garish fluoros or otherwise bold colors designed to snatch the attention of everyone who enters the room or walks the street. And not just the clothes – the practice extends to colored hair, hats, shawls and scarfs which have become equally loud, with the wearers settling for nothing less than complete molestation from every set of eyes in the immediate vicinity.

The Exclamation

The exclamation is timed just as the male target comes into earshot, and is often delivered in the form of a small shock or surprise; "Oh, I nearly fell over!" states the woman into the thin air, or "My goodness its so hot today" in the hopes a perfect stranger will begin gazing in the direction of the voice and, with luck, take up her topic of self-discussion.

The Exclamation can also appear as a muttering about something at just the right moment. This is a favorite and is normally delivered in the form of a question or statement in need of an answer, such as when she is in earshot of the right man in the shopping aisle and frustratedly mutters, supposedly to herself, "I can't find the cans of spaghetti I wonder if they've moved them?" or "I hope they are getting some fresh bread in today!" that the passing male might hear and feel compelled to respond.

Look At Me Strut:

Strutting gorgeously, exuding self-sufficiency with an *I-don't-need-a-man* look, the strutter has mastered the art of *appearing* disinterested in attention, while making a distracting physical display of swinging arms, loudly clopping heels, eye catching attire, and a chin-in-the-air look that begs a second glance from the target males. This routine is generally pulled in central business district where she assiduously scans shopfront windows to capture all those reflected male gazes that her empowered strutting dreams of capturing. Her skill at using shopfront windows to look at both herself and the reflected faces of those gazing at her rises up to an artform that allows her to look sideways and yet not trip over when having little focus on the road ahead.

Exhibit A.

Lyrics for the song Alice Blue Gown

In my sweet little Alice blue gown
When I first wandered down into town
I was so proud inside, 'cause I felt every eye
And in every shop window I primped passing by
A new manner of fashion I'd found
And the world seemed to smile all around
So it wouldn't be proper if made of silk were another
My sweet little Alice blue gown

The Volume Increase

This gaze-puller happens when you are walking toward a woman who happens to be with one or more of her girlfriends and, desiring your gaze to be directed on her like the lazer of a sniper, she suddenly turns up the volume of the conversation she is having, or laughs very loudly, often to the astonishment of her female companion who has not seen its purpose. As ridiculous as she may appear to her friend, she has nevertheless succeeded in attracting those dirty male eyes – even if by a guy simply wondering what that sudden blast of noise was about.

The Accessory

Women utilize accessories to draw attentions – a dog, a handbag, a child, or whatever else is handy. The handbag can be swung around or rummaged through in such a way as to capture the attention of the most sight impaired person in the room. Likewise children can be fawned over, or chastised, just as a target male walks by, where mother will say "Don't let that nice man see you eating candy" or "Don't get in the way of the nice man or you might get hurt." This is not to say that every woman and child who interacts with strangers is seeking the male gaze – many are simply engaging in polite public interaction. But a significant portion of them, perhaps especially single mothers, are soliciting further attentions.

Some women claim the best way to meet a man is to buy a dog and take it for a walk, where you'll meet a handsome man either walking his own dog, or perhaps just walking alone. If it's timed right, she knows her dog will follow the irresistible temptation to interact with the dog belonging to Mr. Handsome, and as a bonus the leashes might become entangled. In this scene she gains his eyes, and hopefully his conversation... will they get married?

Gesturing and Gesticulating

Women seem particularly adept at using physical movements to gain the male gaze. The many movements and postures of the arms, the hand placed strategically on chest, thigh, tummy, and the fingertips extended to touch various parts of the body or face – the chin, lips, cleavage. Or consider the tossing, sweeping, or twirling of the hair, and the flutters, glances or stares of the eyes, all designed to force an interaction from the harvestee.

The Lean In

What Sheryl Sandberg failed to admit was that women have been *leaning in* for millennia – with their cleavage. They do this for precisely the same reasons as Sandberg states – to get a rise, promotion, more money, status, and marriage. Perhaps that's what Sandberg unconsciously understood by that decidedly peculiar body-posture phrase *Lean In* – the old trick of bamboozaling with boobs. Why else would a woman need to "lean" "in"?

However it doesn't only happen in the board room or in the hiring room of the Human Resources officer. It happens equally at the bar, the gym, the music concert and the shopping center, places where women can get an equally good rise without even asking for one, at least not verbally. All she need to is lean in to get the attention she wants.

Did you notice something about these techniques? They are the same ones used by salespeople, like the ones you see selling wares in shopping malls who bounce a balloon up and down, twiddle a pen, or dance as the unsuspecting shopper walks in their direction only to be assaulted by a sideshow of color and movement. But rather than sell a product, the gaze-harvesting woman wants you to undress her with your eyes, a sign that her techniques have wielded power over you for her own narcissistic or material gain.

Next time you find yourself in one of these situations, try grasping some true agency by turning your eyes *away* from the female harvester, and enjoying the comedy when she becomes pissed at your refusal and ups the anti – becoming louder, brighter, faster, and more obstructive as she attempts to salvage her failing effort.

You see, the real lack of agency appears when a man's senses are raped by an uninvited inrush of sensory stimuli, a bombardment arising from someone's selfish designs over where you should be gazing.

References:

[1] Laura Mulvey is credited with coining the phrase 'The Male Gaze' in her 1975 article *Visual pleasure and narrative cinema*.

Hera, Ancient Greek goddess of feminism

The Greek goddess Hera was the patroness of marriage, status, and social power, and as I hope to demonstrate here, a goddess appropriate to feminism too. By analyzing the character of a goddess we follow the late psychologist James Hillman's suggestion that "Mythology is psychology in ancient dress," – ie. it gives us insight into human nature, and more specifically into the nature of feminism.

No other goddess in the Greek pantheon comes close to capturing the activities we associate with feminism – not the warlike independence of the Amazons, not the esteemed motherhood of Demeter, and not the allure of Aphrodite. These are merely peripheral topics taken up by a feminism that is concerned with securing multiple varieties of power, and Hera is the goddess I'm going to finger for that role.

Marriage

Hera was first and foremost a goddess of marriage, or rather *the* goddess of marriage. Under her sign marriage tamed men to great advantage of the Greek State – and the State in turn extended honors to her cult. In parts of Greece men could not be recognized as citizens until the day of their marriage, thus enticing men to marry and providing a means for Greek cities to continue reproducing the citizen-estate – not to mention securing a ready supply of laborers, taxes and military personnel to boot. James Hillman writes,

> Marriage belongs to the state; it belongs to society, to the community. Zeus and Hera are social stability; they are the state in a way, so we can be married by a Justice of the Peace at City Hall, because marriage is also secular. We recognize that by having both church weddings and legal weddings. Our tax code, our inheritance laws acknowledge that a fundamental structure of the organization of society is marriage. Therefore some can claim it has nothing in particular to do with the persons who are engaged; it hasn't anything to do with God; it hasn't anything to do with symbolic representations. It is a fundamental structure of society belonging to the polis or the city or the community.[1]

While the marriage of Hera and Zeus is mythological, life in this instance had a way of imitating art. In the marriage month (*Gamelion*) the mythical marriage of Hera and Zeus was reenacted and celebrated with public festivities, a time when many couples would get married in imitation of the divine couple. On these occasions prayers and offerings were given to Hera, and the bride would pledge fidelity to extending Hera's dominion on earth. One can only surmise that the riches, status, and influence of the divine couple became a model to which each couple would hope to aspire.

Another facet of Hera's cult was the focus on buildings, and her temples were usually the biggest and most lavish in all Greece. Women would carve small houses, or make them out of clay and give as offerings to the Goddess. Remarking on this practice, Hillman states that our modern obsession with houses and real estate, one of the bedrocks of our economy, may also arise from a Hera-like sentiment;

> If you think back to all the times you play house as a child, or had a dollhouse, or made little houses out of cartons and boxes, this is an archetypal move going on. We forget that the house is not just something made by an architect and sold you by a developer... What one does for the house, to the house, with the house, is taking care of Hera. Housekeeping is a Hera activity. Our culture recognizes this. Think of the enormous quantity of house magazines: House and Garden, House Beautiful, Home Decorating, Architectural Digest, World of Interiors, the home section of newspapers, home improvement on TV, supposedly a best-selling TV show or one of the most watched, "This Old House."

> "I know a woman who decorates people's houses. You pick out the furniture and the fabrics – then she'll lay out the paintings you should have, what repros you should have on the wall, and the bric-a-brac and what colors the walls should be and so on. She told me that in every one of the cases that she works with (of married couples), the woman picks out everything in the house and the entire house belongs to her except for the husband's desk and his playroom and maybe the garage. He has his little area and the rest of the house is hers. He makes no decisions about what

color the upholstery should be or the kinds of window shades.

"Often when you go to people's houses the wife shows off the house while the husbands talk shop. "Come, let me show you my house; I want to show you the house." She's showing a part of her Hera nature.

"There are these old sayings (whether you go with the gender of them or not): a woman likes a man who can do things around the house, and she hates it that she always has to pick up after him and he leaves things in a mess. By desecrating the house that way, he insults Hera. And a man likes a woman who's a good housekeeper. These are Hera statements. Another one: She loves the house more than me. And the jokes: A man is making love to a whore and she says, "You're the greatest;" and when he's making love to his mistress, she says, "I love you so much." But when he's making love to his wife, she says: "I wonder what color we should paint the ceiling." Now, that is a nasty gender joke, but it isn't! She really loves the house. That's crucial and shouldn't be treated as just a kind of obsession. Her obsession with the house equals his obsession with sex.[1]

In a telling newspaper cartoon some years ago, two women were conversing. The first said she was getting a divorce, to which her friend replied it must be an awful thing to go through. "Not really" the woman replied, "it's actually a dream come true; I get the house, the furniture, the artworks and the kids. I've been planning this divorce since I was a little girl!" In this cruel cartoon we get a sense that the husband was merely a backdrop to securing the larger vision of a house, renovations, furnishings and the children. But especially the house.

Taming Men

Hera was nicknamed 'The Tamer.' She tamed horses, men and heroes and in some places was recognized as the tamer of the seasons, of nature, and even the universe itself.

Her goal was to limit wildness and freedom by placing all creatures in her service. Her tools-for-taming were the entrapment of men and women in marriage, the use of her own sexuality as an enticement for conformity, shaming, and aggressive punishment of any rebellious behaviours. Even her lordly husband Zeus did not escape her control: "Hera's cruel rage tamed him."[2]

Hera was worshipped as 'Goddess of the yoke,' an enslaving device symbolizing her desire to create utilities of beasts and men. She yoked obedient men to wives, and yoked heroes to an inevitable death through their performance of labours that bring betterment to women and society.

In the Iliad Hera is said to tame heroes through death, not marriage. Death through service to others was considered -and is still considered- something appropriate for males and for their own good. In *The Myth of Male Power* Warren Farrell recounts a Greek story which illustrates the fact:

The Hero As Slave:

Once upon a time, a mother who wanted to see the beautiful statue of Hera had no oxes or horses to carry her there. But she did have two sons. And the sons wanted more than anything to make their mother's wish come true. They volunteered to yoke themselves to a cart and take her over the mountains in the scorching heat to the faraway village of Argos, the home of the statue of Hera (the wife of Zeus). Upon their arrival in Argos, the sons were cheered and statues (that can be found to this day) were built in their honor. Their mother prayed that Hera give her sons the best gift in her power. Hera did that. The boys died. The traditional interpretation? The best thing that can happen to a man is to die at the height of his glory and power. Yet had this been a myth of two daughters who had substituted themselves for oxen to carry their father somewhere, would we have interpreted the daughters' deaths as proof that the best thing that can happen to a woman is to die at the height of her glory and power? The statues and cheers can be seen as bribes for the sons to value their lives less than their mother's request to view a statue. The fact that the statue was of Hera, the queen of the Olympian gods and protector of married women is symbolic. The sons' sacrifice symbolized the mandate for men to become strong enough to serve the needs of mothers and marriage, and to be willing to call it glory if they died in the process. Which is why the name Hercules means "for the glory of Hera".[3]

Sexual manipulation was another of Hera's strategems to gain what she wanted. In one popular tale, for instance, she asked if she could borrow Aphrodite's magic girdle to help her woo the King of the gods. By borrowing Aphrodite's natural charms (the girdle) Hera imitated the goddess of love and sex and thereby seduced Zeus. As we read in Homer's Iliad, the magical girdle of Aphrodite had the power to create subservience in the target;

> Hera was divided in purpose as to how she could beguile the brain in Zeus of the aigis. And to her mind this thing appeared to be the best counsel, to array herself in loveliness, and go down to Ida, and perhaps he might be taken with desire to lie in love with her next her skin, and she might be able to drift an innocent warm sleep across his eyelids, and seal his crafty perceptions...

> Now, when she had clothed her body in all this loveliness, she went out from the chamber, and called aside Aphrodite to come away from the rest of the gods, and spoke a word to her: 'Would you do something for me, dear child... Give me loveliness and desirability, graces with which you overwhelm mortal men, and all the immortals...

> Then in turn Aphrodite the laughing (philomeides) answered her: 'I cannot, and I must not deny this thing that you ask for, you, who lies in the arms of Zeus, since he is our greatest.' She spoke, and from her breasts unbound the

elaborate, pattern-pierced zone (himas), and on it are figured all beguilement (philotes), and loveliness is figured upon it, and passion of sex (himeros) is there, and the whispered endearment (oaristos) that steals the heart away even from the thoughtful. She put this in Hera's hands, and called her by name and spoke to her: 'Take this zone, and hide it away in the fold of your bosom. It is elaborate, all things are figured therein. And I think whatever is your heart's desire shall not go unaccomplished.' So she spoke, and the ox-eyed lady Hera smiled on her and smiling hid the zone away in the fold of her bosom.[4]

Hera employed sexual manipulativeness as an artifice to purchase the power and influence she so desperately craved. Today we would call this behavior "Love bombing," which has the ability to tame a man to schemes he might otherwise have never dreamed of following.

Binding Hera's rage

When Hera didn't get her desired measure of power, when her status didn't reach high enough, or worse, when she *lost* status or power, things went very badly for the world around her. Epithets of spitefulness, jealousy, vengefulness, vindictiveness, cruelty and rage belong to the scorned goddess, and from a reading of the myths it seems she felt scorned much of the time.

We turn for example to the priestess Medea who murdered her children as revenge against her husband's transgressions. Her husband, Jason of Argonauts fame, decided to leave her after the marriage went stale. He found a new bride and Medea devised to make them suffer for their happiness. Much like the goddess Hera to whom Medea was priestess, she carried out a scorched-earth policy in the face of frustrated power urges, saying;

> I will send them with gifts in their hands, carrying them unto the bride a robe of finest woof and a chaplet of gold. And if these ornaments she take and put them on, miserably shall she die, and likewise everyone who touches her; with such fell poisons will I smear my gifts. And here I quit this theme; but I shudder at the deed I must do next; for I will slay the children I have borne… and when I have utterly confounded Jason's house I will leave the land, escaping punishment for my dear children's murder, after my most unholy deed… so help me God, Never shall he see again alive the children I bore to him, nor from his new bride shall he beget issue, for she must die a hideous death, slain by my drugs. Let no one deem me a poor weak woman who sits with folded hands, but of another mould, dangerous to foes and well-disposed to friends.[5]

After killing Jason's bride with a poison-smeared robe, murdering her own children, and then setting fire to the palace, Medea fled to Athens where she married the mighty King Aegeus, thereby securing a place of notoriety in the mythological scheme of Greece.

Mythologist Karl Kerenyi asks, "What should we make of it that Medea, a barbaric representative of the Hera world, and her gloomy cult, found acceptance in the sacred precinct of Zeus' spouse?"[6] Kerenyi was struck by the fact that Hera remained associated with Medea's barbarism and surrounded her with the sanctity of her own world. Our thoughts on this question might extend to a similar comparison of moderate feminism and how it remains associated with radical feminism's relational and cultural terrorism.

The Greeks understood better than we moderns, however, that impulses of the psychopathic mind needed to be restrained by a civil society.

To that end the Greeks developed a religious ritual that involved winding a rope tightly around a statue or effigy of the Goddess Hera, particularly during what they imagined to be her 'unfulfilled' moments. That hog-tying symbolized containment of destructive energies resulting from loss of status or power. Participants understood the binding was of the proverbial 'woman scorned,' a ritual teaching how to deal with such behavior in the lives of mortals.

In contrast to her fulfilled behavior within marriage, when the Queen of Heaven lost her marital station and status, she would tear the social fabric into black confetti. Hera then became monstrous or in some stories started giving birth to monstrous creatures who did her bidding. Jungian psychologist Murray Stein talks to this monstrous side of the goddess;

> This compounding of evil upon evil is an image of Hera in her *Iuno inferna* aspect and energized by a full-blown animus rage and destruction, running amuck through the world, devouring

whomever she can lay her hands on. Hera is in this development a veritable epidemic of pathology.

The ancient cults of Hera showed great foresight and wisdom in "binding" her image during the dangerous periods of her cycle. This was prophylactic against the potentiation of the she-dragon. But what could they have done to prevent this potentiation in the face of the Typhaonian spirit energizing it? Hera's reaction to her experience with Zeus bursts all fetters, for without a full experience of the *Teleia* [fulfillment] aspect of the cycle the bindings on the *infernal* aspect of it cannot possibly hold. Thus we find in the Homeric and classical image of her a Hera Unbound, whose boundlessness knows no limit to destruction. The rhythm inherent in the archetype has been disturbed, and we get a sort of symphony whose rhythm is one long downbeat. The restoration of Hera *Teleia* is an individual and cultural historical project that is still being worked on in our time.[7]

Feminism

The comparisons of Hera and Medea with feminism are unmistakable. The male shaming, intimidation, manipulation, and power-seeking are all there – as are the destructiveness and scorched-earth policy accompanying frustrated goals.

It's no surprise that a Google search for Hera + feminist returns over 80,000 results, and Medea + feminist over

100,000, and the number of feminist orgs, initiatives and editorials paints its own picture.

Along with Hera, Medea is universally recognized as a feminist heroine. As an example of feminist websites promoting her we read, "There is, however, one other role that we twenty-first-century audiences are able to recognize in Medea: that of the feminist pioneer. And the fact that this precursor of the suffragettes is a mythic character dramatized nearly 2,500 years ago by a man is quite astonishing."[8]

The Wikipedia entry for Medea reads, "Medea is widely read as a proto-feminist text to the extent that it sympathetically explores the disadvantages of being a woman in a patriarchal society," – to which characterization is implied (by feminists) that we dare not read her as anything but a hapless victim, as one Jungian analyst Cheryl Fuller was to discover.

Fuller, a feminist, gives a revealing account of what happened when she attempted to shine a light on the dark side of Medea, and by extension of women. She writes;

> Eight years ago as I searched for a dissertation advisor, I ran into a wall with the feminist scholars on the faculty of my university. As soon as I explained that I wanted to write about Medea came the assumption: of course, they said, you will be looking at the patriarchy as the issue in her behavior. And when I replied that indeed I was not going to be looking in that direction, but rather at Medea herself and at the meaning intrinsic to her acts and her story, interest in my

work evaporated and they declined to serve on my committee. Though long a feminist myself, I had been absent from developments in academic feminism. It had escaped my attention that there were "right" ways and "wrong" ways to study women, both real and mythological, and clearly considering Medea as anything other than a victim of the patriarchy was the "wrong" way.

I persisted, found an advisor who could accept my apparently heretical viewpoint and happily explored the character of Medea and developed a description of a Medea complex. But the resistance to considering that Medea could be anything other than a hapless victim of the patriarchy continued to intrigue me and set me to wondering about the meaning of excluding this dark and troubling aspect of her, and by extension all of us, from our understanding of what it is to be human and more specifically a woman. It is this wondering which is the subject of my paper.[9]

In summary, the traditional binding of Hera has failed and her destructive energies are loosed upon the world – to devastating effect. Her bindings began to unravel in the Middle Ages with the advent of an indiscriminate chivalry that saw men worshiping women as pure and infallible vessels, while failing to recognize *and bind* their destructive potentials with reasonable forms of social constraint.

While we continue on our current path the scorched earth policy too will continue… compliments of a vengeful, and power-craving Hera.

References:

[1] James Hillman, 'Hera, Goddess of Marriage' in *Mythic Figures* (2007)
[2] Joan O'Brien, 'The Tamer of Heroes and Horses,' Chapter 6E in *The Transformation of Hera*, (1993)
[3] Warren Farrell, The Myth of Male Power, Simon and Schuster, (1993)
[4] Richard Lattimore, Trans. The Iliad of Homer (1951)
[5] Medea By Euripides (431 B.C.E), Translated by E. P. Coleridge (1891)
[6] Karl Kerenyi, Goddesses of Sun and Moon (1979)
[7] Murray Stein, Hera: Bound and Unbound, in *Spring: an annual of Archetypal Psychology* (1977)
[8] Medea: Everywoman, Many Women (website)
[9] Cheryl Fuller, Medea, Feminism and the Shadow (2009)

Feminism, sex-differences and chivalry

On which side should the men's movement focus its activism -— on the similarities or differences between the sexes?

The thinkers among us will stay abreast of both sides of the argument, however in the realm of activism most will take up a position one way or the other to make their point.

Arguments for sameness or difference rest on a more fundamental dyad, the biological and cultural – topics that have been tackled extensively in manosphere discussion circles, though I'm not sure we have gained good mileage from them in the fight against gynocentrism.

Regardless of whether we fixate on biological imperatives, or on the biology-shaping power of culture, the gender war rages on unchecked.[1]

So just for a moment, let's partition-out the hard scientific discussions of biology vs. culture, and pay more attention to the *rhetorical* leverage points of sexual politics – to those emotive generalizations about sameness/difference. All feminist reasoning, all female privilege, and all misandry start from there.

Departing from the usual MRA emphasis on differences, real and significant biological ones, this article will make a case for focusing on the *similarities*, on the things men and women have in common as the most effective basis for relativizing gynocentrism. Emphasizing only differences between the sexes, as old-school men's rights advocates like to do, will not reach the goal of countering feminist propaganda and the anti-male culture created by same. Let's look at some rationale for this move.

Difference Feminism as the order of the day

> I am here going to chart three changes within socialist feminism over the last fifteen years. It has, I argue, moved in large part from androgyny to gender difference, and from Marxism or revolutionary socialism towards an accommodation with, if reform of, the political and social system we know now. [2]

In this quote, feminist Judith Evans makes an observation many are familiar with; that today's feminism is more concerned with promoting sexual differences than androgyny. While obvious to astute observers, I will argue that feminist ideology and feminist activism has not traveled in a linear fashion from androgyny to gynocentrism as Evans suggests, but more accurately has always enjoyed it both ways.

Ernest B. Bax observed this fact well over a century ago:

> "Modern Feminism would fain achieve the feat of eating its cake and having it too. When political and economic rights are in question, such as

involve gain and social standing, the assumption of inferiority magically disappears before the strident assertion of the dogma of the equality of woman with man – her mental and moral equality certainly! When, however, the question is of a different character – for example, for the relieving of some vile female criminal of the penalty of her misdeeds-then Sentimental Feminism comes into play, then the whole plaidoyer is based on the chivalric sentiment of deference and consideration for poor, weak woman." [Chapter V: The "Chivalry" Fake, in *The Fraud of Feminism* 1913]

"Feminists only claim equality with men in so far as it has agreeable consequences for women. And this applies all along the line... I would advise woman's-righters to choose the one side or the other. If they stick to the weakness of woman physically as ground for woman's privileges and immunities, let them give up prating of equality otherwise. If they contend for equality let it at least be an even equality all round." ['Female Suffrage' – in *Social Democrat*, Vol.8, no.9, pp.533-545 1904].

"The bulk of the advocates of woman's rights are simply working, not for equality, but for female ascendency. It is all very well to say they repudiate chivalry. They are ready enough to invoke it politically when they want to get a law passed in their favour – while socially, to my certain knowledge, many of them claim it as a right every whit as much as ordinary women."

['No Misogyny But True Equality' – in *To-day*, pp.115-121 1887]

Reading through Bax's articles it's clear that feminists argued in both directions, especially enjoying the *difference* narrative, proving that sentimental appeals to sex-difference were the approach that gained women the most. Why?

Because differences, especially those implying weakness and vulnerability, evoke chivalry.
And chivalry brings goodies!

Men's advocates need to catch up with this fact and realize that whenever we promote difference, be it biological or cultural in origin, we play into feminist word-games and provide them with the basis for arguing chivalric treatment for women.

Commentaries on men and women's different natures and the corollary of why men and women should be treated differently (read *special treatments for women*) appear throughout history. The claims are that men and women are different due to cultural training (e.g. men are trained in patriarchy and violence; women in softness and subservience), or they are biologically different (e.g. men are testosterone poisoned, and women give birth and need special help), thus, we must discriminate to better serve those differences, say feminists.

Whenever old school MRAs thrash their swords around yelling "WE ARE BIOLOGICALLY DIFFERENT!!" they play right into the rhetoric and remedies of feminists. In fact, many of the more prominent stars in the MRM specialize in promoting difference, arguing for biological differences over culturally implanted ones, and not realizing that they end up with a conclusion of *difference* that gets exploited equally by feminists – it matters not whether the difference is of cultural or biological origin.

Conversely, when we discuss that men and women have a massive overlapping area of shared humanity – the discussion changes to one of equal value, concern and empathy for men.

Males and females, for example, are both among the homeless, both are among the mentally ill, both can be poor or disabled. Men and women equally experience all emotions- jealousy, pride, elation, fear, anxiety, depression, or joy, and they equally suffer heart attacks, diabetes, strokes, broken bones, malaria or the common cold. Both suffer the impact of environmental degradation and pollution, and so on.

Despite that massive area of overlap, you can already read the "difference" argument being exploited by protofeminist Modesta Pozzo in the year 1590;

> Don't we see that men's rightful task is to go out to work and wear themselves out trying to accumulate wealth, as though they were our factors or stewards, so that we can remain at home like the lady of the house directing their work and enjoying the profit of their labors? That, if you like, is the reason why men are naturally stronger and more robust than us — they need to be, so

they can put up with the hard labor they must endure in our service."[3]

And it doesn't stop with Pozzo. The same language can be seen by virtually all feminist writers from her day to the present, including revered feminist philosophers like Julia Kristeva or Iris M. Young, through to the "difference feminists" of today. The historical lineup, all milking difference, is unbroken.

Take for instance the language of popular "equity" feminist Christina Hoff-Sommers who, while helpfully deconstructing many feminist myths, is happy to promote sex-differences as a basis for seeking chivalry for women:

Sommers demonstrates the sex-differences perspective in an interview with Emily Esfahani Smith. "Chivalry is grounded in a fundamental reality that defines the relationship between the sexes," explains Sommers, "and given that most men are physically stronger than most women, men can overpower women at any time to get what they want." "If women give up on chivalry, it will be gone," says Sommers, and "If boys can get away with being boorish, they will, happily. Women will pay the price."[4]

The historical benefit to women of the *difference* argument has far outweighed the sameness argument because difference enlists the traditions of damselling, white knighting, and romantic chivalry. The *sameness* argument fails to tap into those medieval powers and thus affords far less reach for gynocentric tentacles.

* * *

Feminists are among the most rigid enforcers of gender stereotypes on the planet – all while championing "varieties of masculinities/femininities" which "don't fit the binary." However, those varieties are something they tend to spout for window dressing, in passing, before going on to enforce strict gender stereotypes in most everything they say.

Some MRAs miss the fact that many feminists today are *difference feminists* or *cultural feminists* – feminists who believe first and foremost in reinforcing real or perceived differences between men and women. Many of us labor under the assumption that feminists promote a polymorphous perverse (androgynous) identity — *which they never did with any consistency.*

And for feminists it doesn't matter if the differences are of biological origin (many feminists subscribe to Evolutionary psychology) or the result of cultural conditioning – selling any differences of sexed behavior allows them to argue for special treatments for women and harsh treatment for men, regardless of whether the differences are congenital or cultural.

As advocates for men, we would do well to emphasize the biological/behavioral overlap between the sexes – that we all feel emotions, all think, fall in love, catch a common cold, and seek intimate human bonds – and with that we can defeat calls for preferential treatments of women arising from differences. Let's move on from the task of defeating 'feminist androgyny,' which appears to be an activism dead-end.

This article contends that some men's advocates place the focus on differences between men and women and that such an approach is an activism cul-de-sac. But before adopting the alternative strategy of highlighting male and female behavioral similarities, we need first to observe how feminists have used the difference narrative to their advantage; only then will we see the urgency.

So next time you see an argument for difference or sameness, stop and ask yourself who stands the greatest chance of benefiting from it. And if you are advocating for *difference*, ask yourself if you are helping to promote men's human rights or instead promoting a return to the good-ol-days of strictly demarcated gender roles.

References:

[1] Joseph Henrich, *The Secret of Our Success: How Culture Is Driving Human Evolution, Domesticating Our Species, and Making Us Smarter*, Princeton University Pres, 2013
[2] Judith Evans, *Socialist Feminism: From Androgyny to Gynocentrism, Equality to Difference* – 1995
[3] Modesta Pozzo, *The Worth of Women: their Nobility and Superiority to Men* – 1590
[4] Emily Esfahani Smith, 'Let's Give Chivalry Another Chance' The Atlantic, Dec 10 2012.
For more on Hoff-Sommers' views on chivalry, see "The Acculturated Podcast: Ladies and Gentlemen"

Feminism's love affair with gender differences

1. GYNOCENTRISM (Greek: γυνή, "female" –
Latin: centrum, "centred")
■ (a). n. Dominant or exclusive focus on women in
theory or practice; or to the advocacy of this. Often
practiced to the detriment of non-females.

PragerU are being very intelligent about how they peddle
their version of chivalry and service to the damsels. Some
years ago, they approached us on face book to run some
of their "Man up and get married" material.

Blunt and rude story short, we said "No!"

They now have a much more insidious program going
forward to incentivize young boys to run to the plantation
in gynocentric service.

It is our belief they intend to make good gains for
traditional gynocentrism out of the work of the men's
rights movement and antifeminism over the last decade
and that is definitely not in the best interests of men and
boys.

In this recent video by PragerU we have a neotenous
blonde woman pearl-clutching over violence against
women as if she was a feminist... but coming at it from
the traditionalist perspective. Listen for the incongruous
statements, opening with, "It is now OK for a man to hit a

woman!" appearing on to the screen calling you to fight to protect the ladies.

Core to making this approach work is the highlighting of the *differences* between men and women and blaming feminism for the similarities argument. "The sexes are different. Marvel at it, enjoy it."

We all know that feminism is a manifestation of unbridled gynocentricty and that's a bad thing right? We all know they like to talk about fish on bicycles and fantasize that women can do anything a man can do, better, backwards and in heels.

Men and women have similar talents is their theme.

So it must follow that any argument describing the obvious differences between the two genders must be a good thing right?

Well, not so fast pal. While Occam's Razor is a very useful tool, it's not a universal law and reality is often a good bit more complicated than our initial summation of it.

The map is never the territory.

Men and women are far more alike than they are different, a no-brainer when we consider that around 99% of our genetic code is identical. Humans however seem to highlight and at times exaggerate gender differences, which may be an evolutionary strategy to get us to notice potential mates.

To be clear there are important differences between males and females, but there is no incompatibility between the idea of low sexual dimorphism and data we do have on the differences. Male variability is real for example but most noticeable at the extremes of any data set, and more broadly noticeable in physical and hormonal differences.

At the more subtle level minor biological differences between the sexes could give rise to significantly different results (emergent behaviour). Men and women tend to seek out different types of work. The underlying differences that cause this may be slight when compared to the set of motivations that drive a person but it turns out to be significant to us when we look at societies.

The occasional feminist can be seen to propose that there's no such thing as sexual dimorphism, arguing instead that gender is only a social construct. But to place all feminists into this category is to create a strawman, one frequently appealed to by those who would have us return to a more traditional gynocentric vision of "biology based" gender roles – he labors outside the home, she bakes apple pies in the kitchen. While the overly-simplified charge that feminists "promote sameness" may be seductive, it likely comes with the entrapping antidote of traditional gynocentric gender roles.

To be sure feminists have played the debate both ways – sometimes arguing gender is a result of social construction, and just as often arguing for biology as the basis for our differences. The undeniable fact is all three waves of feminism have evoked women's smaller physical size, lower strength, pregnancy and lactation, unique endocrinology, reproductive system, menstruation, breast health, vagina health etc as reasons for special dispensations (chivalry) in the form of less labour, more comfort, more protection, and more health services (eg. the many 'women's hospitals,' safe-spaces, special seating at venues, financial considerations, and so on). Feminists have always promoted biological differences, or rather *exploited* them, and their more recent infiltration into the field of Evolutionary Psychology will only serve to strengthen that trend.

The point we are making is that whether they are biological, sociological or both in origin, the laboring of difference has allowed feminists to win the day because difference garners chivalry – sameness garners no chivalry. Chivalry got us into this goddam mess.

Difference garners chivalry – sameness garners no chivalry

Let that sink in. If we are ever to defeat gynocentrism, it will require a weakening of the appeal to chivalry, which will require a weakening of the appeal to difference by both feminists and traditional gynocentrists alike. If we ever succeed in that goal it will make room for the reality of equality. Equality of opportunity, not the equality of outcome that the feminists so often push for.

And true equality means a step down for women.

Chivalry must die. Entirely.

For chivalry to die, the mechanism for it must be recognised and replaced. And the underlying mechanism for chivalry is the difference between the sexes.

Marc Rudov, one of the most powerful voices ever to speak on gendered issues, was very clear on this as he understood it implicitly:

> I've recently published a book about women and know them well. My true education in all things feminine began almost 12 years ago, when I became reimmersed in the single world after my divorce. During this post-marriage odyssey with the "opposite" sex, I learned that women are not so opposite and are, in fact, much like men. To me, this is no longer a debate; it is fact. Now, we hear almost daily from anthropologists, psychiatrists, psychologists, licensed psychotherapists, so-called life coaches, movies, books, magazines, TV, radio, parents, friends, lovers, and standup comics that men and women are wired differently and hopelessly incompatible. We are coached to accept, embrace, and gingerly navigate these differences. Nonsense, I say. If you believe this propaganda, you are part of the problem."

> "If you're honest with yourself, you cannot find many real differences between men and women. The differences you've always thought about are socialized differences based on myths. If women were as different and mythical as the so-called experts would have you believe, they'd never be able to run major corporations, cities, states, and

nations. When we stop behaving according to our socialized programming, our stereotypical roles, we are surprisingly similar. This behavioral shift is the solution for making our romances more harmonious and successful.[1]

The primary difference we regularly point to in justification of chivalry is physical size and strength. But man created hydraulics for a reason.

For example, and extremely heavy, hand held 'pounding tool' was once the way a man compacted soil in the construction of roads.

Today, however, we use gas-propelled roller vehicles with easy to operate power steering.

Women can drive these things.
Women can now construct roads.
Women are the same as men.
Women are equal.

Yes, buttercups, you do have to get up in the cold and dark and go outside to work in the dust and flies, eat your lunch in a construction pit and come home in the dark.

Welcome to equality.
Mind your step down.

In Australia we have a female icon, a truck driver hauling massive loads on dusty outback roads, who understood this equality issue better than any woman. Her name was Toots Holzheimer and she lived and died in the man's world of disposability. She had no truck with a badge of feminist power princess, wonder woman, or traditional victim damsel being pushed by PragerU. Just straight up equality.

Feminism and chivalry have always functioned as a gestalt, as Ernest B. Bax observed over a century ago when he referred to first-wavers as "chivalry feminists." The feminist emphasis on gender differences, especially those implying weakness and vulnerability, evokes chivalry which is then used as a leverage point to secure multiple varieties of power from men in positions of power. The win gained by this ruse ensures feminists and traditional gynocentric women enjoy a quasi-aristocratic status above the rest of society – hence why feminists are usually seen to be comfortable middle to upper-class white women.

Discussions about differences will always result in special treatment for women, and that always means disposability for men. Alternatively, when we discuss that men and women have a massive overlapping area of shared humanity the discussion potentially changes to one of equal value, concern and empathy for men.

The Men's Rights Movement

Neither A Voice for Men (website) nor Men's Rights in general is about promoting traditional gynocentrism. Anything that is based in the statement, "Women will pay an especially high price…" is not central to the AVfM mission. Our mission is centered on the male price being paid in an essentially misandric, gynocentric world.

That does not mean we deny that women have issues that stem from their gender nor that those problems should be bereft of compassion. Rather we recognize that both sexes have their own issues that must be addressed in human terms and compassion rather than through a sexist and mono-gendered paradigm as guides the current misandric system of male disposability, absent of compassion for men and boys.

At AVfM we do recognise many men will always seek the companionship of and sexual contact with women, no matter how much bleating the monk MGTOWs want to do to berate us for recognizing it.

And that's the danger of Prager and their slippery sales pitch to traditionalist-leaning men.

It's too deliciously small of a step to gain recognized "manhood," along with admiration and perhaps sexual intimacy for many to resist jumping on the wagon back to the plantation where they will gain their social value and identity in service and sacrifice to the women folk – women who long ago shucked some if not all of the traditional roles that might have gone part of the way to creating a reciprocal exchange.

After all, what more noble cause is there for a man to take? Indeed, what nobler path is there to real manhood? Our answer to that is one where you're not selling your soul in the hope of sexual gratification and a Pyrrhic validation of your masculine worth.

Try some service where you're not trading in the shallow hope of being paid in sweaty endorphins while attempting to force all other men into this deal with the devil and a straight jacket definition of masculinity.

There is no nobility there at all.

They will do nothing for men and boys beyond erecting monuments to those who died in service to women. What they mean to take from those males has no limit. All for a social construct of what it means to be a man. A real man.

And this epitaph will be used as a weapon of shame against any boy with the intellect to question the paradigm of Mayan sacrificial service.

To ensure the sun rises, you must die! Your beating heart must be torn out! Man and boy!

Male disposability as an artifact of the past

Male disposability has a basis in evolutionary theory. When the females of a species invest significantly more energy in to gestation than males, as is the case for humans, then the size of the next generation is largely constrained by the number of fertile females. As a result of this a species can generally tolerate the loss of males more easily than the loss of females. The loss of females will constrain the size of the next generation, the loss of males will constrain genetic diversity.

We humans are now a special case. The Earth carries more than 7.5 billion people today and could be carrying 10 or 11 billion within a few decades. We no longer need the ability to rapidly recover numbers, thus any presumed bias towards male disposability that existed in the past no longer needs to apply. Likewise encouraging women to have babies is an equally retrograde message to those who are making the conscious decision to stop overpopulating the planet.

There are numerous other differences. For example women retain more neotenous characteristics from their childhood than do men. The reasons for this are outside the scope of this article other than to point out that the "reproductive bottleneck" mentioned earlier shows that men benefited from protecting women in pre-modern times. That women would retain child-like characteristics that encouraged men to do this seems self-evident.

To put these sex differences in context we can say that men and women have, as outlined above, more in common than they have in difference, a fact which makes the PragarU-style obsession with difference look all the more pressed. The gender similarities hypothesis as defined by researchers holds that males and females are similar on most, but not all, psychological variables. That is, men and women, as well as boys and girls, are more alike than they are different. A gender similarities hypothesis does not assert that males and females are similar in absolutely every domain. The exceptions— areas in which gender differences are moderate or large in magnitude should equally be recognized.[2]

While the 'gender similarities hypothesis' reviews meta-analyses of multiple studies on gender differences, it is prone to methodological biases like any other research. For example proponents of the hypothesis sometimes understate the extent of gender differences when they do appear,[3] or may otherwise omit factors such as gender differences in the human brain; gender and sex hormones; or gender differences in physical health/illness in their analysis. By and large though it is usually easy to separate the baby from the bathwater.

On the subject of differences, the biological necessity of male disposability is an artifact of the past and that's where it should stay. PragerU has no urgent basis to encourage a return to the plantation for species survival, nor to promote the associated grinding of male lives to dust in the service of the uterus that involves the consequent, necessary lack of compassion for male pain and loss that characterized early hominid societies.

Watching the slickness of their operation, they don't strike me as being slow between the intellectual wickets. It's not in the scope of this article to enter the field of global conspiracies, but suffice to say, where many of you see countries, we see farms with human livestock.

Disposability does require a solid breeding program. There's money in them there breeders.

So who wants to man up?

References:

[1] Marc Rudov, Five Myths About Women
[2] Janet Hyde, *The Gender Similarities Hypothesis* (2005), and *Gender Similarities and Differences* (2014).
[3] Alastair Davies & Todd K Shackelford, *An evolutionary psychological perspective on gender similarities and differences* (2006)

Mythologies of men's rights and feminist movements

Have you ever thought of Men's Rights and feminism as competing mythologies? In what follows I will do just that, while paying special attention to the fact that the feminist myth has triumphed in capturing global imagination. By 'mythology' I mean those guiding stories that provide meaning and direction to the lives of all who follow them, including the men's rights story, and the feminist story. While myth may or may not be scientifically true, it is true in the sense that people actively believe in myths and act them out in their daily lives.

In his 4-volume work[1] surveying the history of world mythologies, Joseph Campbell gives a snapshot of the evolving history of mythology from the earliest days of 'Master Bear god' painted on cave walls, until the present day.

Campbell demonstrates that, over and over, dominant mythologies get replaced or absorbed by newer mythologies, and such changeability appears to be the only constant in the long sweep of history. There were periods of mythological stability in all cultures, but without exception every traditional mythology was modified or replaced as forces within the culture reached critical mass.

Catalysts for myth revisions are numerous, with examples being foreign invaders who overrun a traditional culture and implant their own mythology, or alternatively it may happen that a new mythology lurking in the back waters of a culture begins to gain grassroots appreciation, leading eventually to its ascendancy and a concomitant decline of the previous mythological setup. By yet another route the change in mythology may be instituted by a ruler who adopts a new religious belief and then mandates it as the official belief of the masses, examples being;

- Indian King Ashoka promoted Buddhist mythology across ancient Asia;
- Emperor Constantine promoted the Christian story as religion of the Roman Empire;
- Queen Eleanor of Aquitaine and her daughter crafted the mythos of romantic love and chivalry which was disseminated throughout Europe and the world.

In some situations the dominant myths did not give way to a revision for a considerable time, usually because there wasn't a compelling mythology jostling to replace it. Even when the prevailing mythology has become somewhat stale and uninspiring, the human mind will not reject it in favor of a story vacuum: to be without some kind of guiding mythology leads the human mind into an existential paralysis, and for the most part nature refuses to tolerate such a void.

Now lets consider all of this in the light of feminism, a movement crafted from florid imaginings of the mythic imagination. To get to the heart of this myth we need to start at the medieval beginnings of those accreted layers of story that constitute the end product we know as modern feminism.

In his volume Creative Mythology,[2] Campbell documents how stories of chivalry and romantic love during the Middle Ages formed a new mythology that not only competed with the Christian religion for social legitimacy, but eventually surpassed it. Today romantic love saturates popular media, song, cinema, dance and the arts, and is the number one selling genre of literature, outselling the books of traditional religion, ie., the Qu'ran, Bible, Vedas, Bhagavad Gita, Tipiṭaka, Tao Te Ching and so on. Romantic love is, as Campbell states, the world's current leading mythos.

So what does all this have to do with men's rights and feminism?

Well, everything.

Feminists freely admit that chivalry and romantic love form ground zero of the feminist enterprise, constituting something of a Genesis Story of women's improved social position, pedestalization and ongoing increases in power. As told by feminist Dr. Elizabeth Reid Boyd of the School of Psychology and Social Science at Edith Cowan University, romance writings can be called the "first form of feminism":

"I muse upon arguments that romance is a form of feminism. Going back to its history in the Middle Ages and its invention by noblewomen who created the notion of courtly love, examining its contemporary popular explosion and the concurrent rise of popular romance studies in the academy that has emerged in the wake of women's studies, and positing an empowering female future for the genre, I propose that reading and writing romantic fiction is not only personal escapism, but also political activism.

Romance has a feminist past that belies its ostensible frivolity. Romance, as most true romantics know, began in medieval times... Love songs and stories, like those of Lancelot and Guinevere, Tristan and Isolde, were soon on the lips of troubadours and minstrels all over Europe. Romance spread rapidly. It has been called the first form of feminism."[3]

Reid Boyd, like so many other feminists before her, makes clear that romantic-love mythology provides bedrock for the development of feminism. Faced with that fantastical adversary, men's advocates can argue they have excellent data demonstrating a growing narcissism among women and a neglect of men, facts that should lead right-thinking people away from the grip of feminism. However, those facts are only in the beginning stages of being woven into a story, one that might, in time, become an epic like the Bible or Mahābhārata.

Axiom: ONLY STORY CAN DISPLACE OR ABSORB OTHER STORIES.

Facts be damned.

Until a new mythology rises to challenge the hegemony of feminist myth, non-gynocentric men are destined to wander the planet like lost souls in search of a place to call home. For many men, the dominant mythology of our time has erased our story, and with it our existence in the world. Campbell talks to this problem when he declared *"Myths are public dreams, dreams are private myths,"* concluding that when your personal understanding of life doesn't align with the dominant public myth, your path in life will be painful:

> *"If your private myth, your dream, happens to coincide with that of the society, you are in good accord with your group. If it isn't, you've got a long adventure in the dark forest ahead of you."*[4]

While that sums up the experience of red-pill men today, all is not lost. A growing number of voices have declared the mythology of feminism overripe for change, that it is rotting to the core as a guide to civilization, and there are in fact compelling stories poised to replace it. Before we look at alternative stories that have potential to help men and women live more harmoniously, lets first survey how the feminist mythos coincides with other mythological traditions.

As with the great civilization-building and sustaining mythologies of the past, feminism has narrated; 1. an Eden story of how ancient men and women co-existed and organized their society; 2. a fall from grace, 3. a set of laws to guide humans away from their fallen ways, and 4. liberation and future utopia.

Each of these four elements, which could be expanded to dozens more, appear in feminist mythology as follows:

1. Once upon a time, much of European society was matriarchal, peace-loving, agrarian, and Goddess worshiping, with men serving as the labor force.[5,6]
2. Patriarchal tribes from the North invaded and suppressed this idyllic Eden, supplanting it with a hierarchical, patriarchal, and woman-oppressing culture.[5,6]
3. Proto-feminists of the Middle Ages, followed by modern feminists, rebelled and challenged the grip of 'the patriarchy' and its institutions to allow women out of the wilderness and into the center of society. They created romantic love, and instituted laws, one by one, that would not only give women equal power to men, but would "compensate" women for previous losses of power.
4. Women would once again rule, as a female aristocracy, with men learning to be obedient, loving and dutiful servants, inaugurating a golden age.[7]

While these beliefs sound fanciful to the rational mind, they are documented and widely believed myths underpinning the feminist movement. With the enormous currency of feminist mythology in modern society, it constitutes 'the story' that we are all, to some extent, 'in.'

Indeed there's no outside of mythological perspectives — culturally we are all living inside them in one way or another. Those of us with a bent for factual accuracy prefer to align with stories that are truer to science, with narratives that are compatible with the facts without departing from them as myths often do. But whether we enjoy them, or rail against them as childish fantasies, the fact is that mythologies full of kooky flat-earth ideas have guided civilizations for millennia without being based on facts at all, and yet the societies they governed continued to flourish regardless.

Mythologies clearly don't need to be factually correct to guide societies. They need only provide a shared operating system that glues people's otherwise separate minds into one harmonious whole.

Those of us with a penchant for scientific fact can hope that a new mythology incorporates more factual data than the flat-earth science of the current gynocentric mythos — one eminently more suited to the scientific age in which we live, and one that many more people could believe in.

To prepare ourselves for inevitable new mythologies, it helps to first become aware of the dominant myths already governing our society. And as Gianni Vattimo once advised, the post-modern paradox of social-mythology is to wake up and realize that we have been dreaming, and yet continue dreaming anyway;[8] ie. we realize we still need stories to live by but we can *consciously* choose the guiding narratives we wish to align with instead of going along with them unconsciously.

As men's rights advocates, that raises questions about our own 'mythologies.' What are they? Have we sufficiently developed and articulated them? In light of the four elements of religious mythology listed above, lets list a rudimentary, rough sketch of the MR story to date. Before I do that, I hasten to add that this sketch is not prescriptive and may be at odds with narratives already held by devout Christian, Muslim, or XYZ-believing MRAs. However this mythological sequence focuses solely on the gender relations problem as it has been articulated by many MRAs today:

1. A strong candidate for an MR 'Genesis story' is the story of human evolution, a compelling mythology about our remote past and how we clawed our way out of the jungle to build the wonders of modern science and civilization. That story comes with scientific observations and anecdotes about human biology in action – how early men and women displayed different sexual and survival strategies, and how human offspring were protected due to biological imperatives. Its a

story of cooperation between men and women as they dreamed the human adventure forward.

2. The 'fall' took place as that delicate equilibrium between men and women was unraveled by the arrival of the new gender relations mythology called romantic chivalry, AKA gynocentrism. This period marked the moment of enslavement to a sexual relations model designed to tilt maximum power to women, with men slaving as Moses did for the Egyptians, and it presided over the destruction of the delicate family unit.

3. Over the centuries men (and women) of iron will and good conscience mounted a resistance to gynocentrism and a desire for Exodus – to wanting to walk away from gynocentric-feminism as free men;

4. Finally, men and women began to live the GOOD NEWS of the MR Testament: liberty, equality of opportunity, compassion and multi-options for all – this time including men.

These four sub-narratives form a larger corpus that we might call a mythology, one that would improve on the current toxic mythos of feminism. As mentioned it is given for illustrative purposes only and is not prescriptive; any new mythology will arise organically like a nighttime dream and flourish within the culture, and like dreams we never know when it will arrive or exactly what shape it will take. But the dream, the myth, will arrive…. of that we can be sure.

If we continue to expand this collection of stories, elaborating them in greater depth, continuing to tell them, and telling them again, more compelling with each recitation, then just maybe our society will have a necessary stone to jump to.

References:

[1] Joseph Campbell, *Masks of God* (4 volume series) (1959 – 1968)
[2] Joseph Campbell, *Creative Mythology*, volume 4 of *Masks of God* series (1968)
— *Occidental Mythology*, volume 3 of *Masks of God* series (1959)
— *Transformations of Myth Through Time*, (1988)
[3] Elizabeth Reid Boyd, *Romancing feminism: From women's studies to women's fiction* (2014)
[4] Joseph Campbell, *The Power of Myth* (1988)
[5] Cynthia Eller, *The Myth of Matriarchal Prehistory: Why an Invented Past Won't Give Women a Future*, (2001)
[6] Lucy Goodison, *Ancient Goddesses*, (1999)
[7] Peter Wright, *A new Aristocracy*, published at gynocentrism.com, (2018)
[8] Richard Kearney, *Poetics of Imagining: Modern to Post-modern* (1998)

Can women be chivalrous? Damn right they can.

Is male chivalry attractive to most women? According to a recent study the answer is, unsurprisingly, *yes.*

A 2013 study on benevolent sexism by Matthew D. Hammond of the University of Auckland[1] found that a high sense of entitlement disposes women to endorse chivalric customs, for example that women need to be protected, cared for and pampered by males.

Hammond and his colleagues had more than 4,400 men and women complete psychological evaluations to measure their sense of entitlement and adherence to sexist beliefs about women. The beliefs included statements such as, "Women should be cherished and protected by men" and "Women, compared to men, tend to have a superior moral sensibility."[2]

This group of individuals was tested again one year later. The researchers found a sense of entitlement in women was associated with stronger endorsement of benevolent sexism. Women who believed they deserved more out of life (and who likely received more out of life) were more likely to endorse benevolent sexist beliefs and their adherence to these beliefs increased over time. The association between a sense of entitlement in men and endorsement of benevolent sexism was weak, by contrast, and did not increase over time.

These findings provide evidence that female-benefiting sexism practiced by women is responsible for sexist attitudes toward their own gender, as well as toward men — attitudes which contribute more broadly to the maintenance of gender stereotypes and inequality on both sides of the fence.

The relationship between narcissism and chivalry

In the study narcissistic attitudes of women are underlined as the motivation to garner resource-attainments and self-enhancements via the generosity of male chivalry. Some of the core features of narcissism include an inflated sense of self-worth; need for praise, admiration, and social status; an undeserved sense of entitlement; a sense that one deserves nice things; and a belief in one's superior intelligence and beauty – all without a commensurate level of validity or deservedness. These features appear to go hand in hand with the expectation of chivalric treatment from others.

A woman (or man) with narcissistic disposition seeks to gain status and resources by fair means or foul, including by charm, feigning confidence, and an energetic approach to social interactions. She will take personal responsibility for all successes that come her way, while attributing all personal failures to external sources – most likely men. Narcissistic traits ensure that the individual will act selfishly to secure material gains even when it means exploiting others, and those practicing benevolent sexism tend to encourage such behaviour. According to the authors:

"Benevolent sexism facilitates the capacity to gain material resources and complements feelings of deservingness by promoting a structure of intimate relationships in which men use their access to social power and status to provide for women (Chen et al., 2009). Second, benevolent sexism reinforces beliefs of superiority by expressing praise and reverence of women, emphasizing qualities of purity, morality, and culture which make women the ''fairer sex.'' Indeed, identifying with these kinds of gender-related beliefs (e.g., women are warm) fosters a more positive self-concept (Rudman, Greenwald, & McGhee, 2001).

Moreover, for women higher in psychological entitlement, benevolent sexism legitimizes a self-centric approach to relationships by emphasizing women's special status within the intimate domain and men's responsibilities of providing and caring for women. Such care involves everyday chivalrous behaviors, such as paying on a first date and opening doors for women (Sarlet et al., 2012; Viki et al., 2003), to more overarching prescriptions for men's behavior toward women, such as being ''willing to sacrifice their own well-being'' to provide for women and to ensure women's happiness by placing her ''on a pedestal'' (Ambivalent Sexism Inventory; Glick & Fiske, 1996)...

In contrast to the overt benefits that benevolent sexism promises women, men's endorsement of benevolent sexism reflects making sacrifices for women by relinquishing power in the relationship domain and providing for and protecting their partners (Glick & Fiske, 1996). Moreover, although benevolent sexism portrays men as ''gallant protectors'' (Glick & Fiske, 2001), it does not emphasize men's superiority over women or cast men as deserving of praise and provision.'' [3]

Judging by the above study we can conclude that women's expectation of chivalric treatment has altered little over the course of the last 800 years since chivalric responsibilities were first instituted. For example we can take the voices of two women from history who give a traditional voice to the findings of the study; the first is by female author Lucrezia Marinella who in 1600 wrote:

"Women are honored everywhere with the use of ornaments that greatly surpass men's, as can be observed. It is a marvelous sight in our city to see the wife of a shoemaker or butcher or even a porter all dressed up with gold chains round her neck, with pearls and valuable rings on her fingers, accompanied by a pair of women on either side to assist her and give her a hand, and then, by contrast, to see her husband cutting up meat all soiled with ox's blood and down at heel, or loaded up like a beast of burden dressed in rough cloth, as porters are. At first it may seem an astonishing anomaly to see the wife dressed like a lady and the husband so basely that he often appears to be her servant or butler, but if we consider the matter properly, we find it reasonable because it is necessary for a woman, even if she is humble and low, to be ornamented in this way because of her natural dignity and excellence, and for the man to be less so, like a servant or beast born to serve her."

Or from another woman <u>Modesta Pozzo</u> who wrote this in 1590:

"For don't we see that men's rightful task is to go out to work and wear themselves out trying to accumulate wealth, as though they were our factors or stewards, so that we can remain at home like the lady of the house directing their work and enjoying the profit of their labors? That, if you like, is the reason why men are naturally stronger and more robust than us — they need to be, so they can put up with the hard labor they must endure in our service.

Chivalry today continues to be understood as a strictly male obligation toward female beneficiaries. In the past however it appears there were *some* exceptions showing that the attribution "chivalry" could be applied equally to any women who demonstrated it. From a search of published literature several examples of female chivalry do appear, such as the following with dates and search-terms in bold/italics:

Female chivalry

<u>1792</u> "Mr. Burke remarked, that however the spirit of chivalry may be in the decline amongst men, the age of *female chivalry* was just commencing."

<u>1918</u> "Spenser, following Ariosto, laments the decay of *female chivalry* since the days of Penthesilia, Deborah, and Camilla."

<u>1938</u> "This tendency among women of making concessions to men for their inferior moral strength I would like to term "*female chivalry*." It is chivalry in the strictest sense of the term because it makes concessions for the weakness of the opposite side. In a society which is so primitive that its women have not yet developed in their conduct with men this moral chivalry, no doubt the woman is an inferior and subordinate member, an object of masculine pity. But the moment she brings into play upon the field of our social behaviour her superior moral strength (manifested through the developments of her inherent powers of sacrifice, endurance and self-discipline) she not only qualifies herself for equality of treatment but records a moral victory of first magnitude over the opposite sex."

Woman's chivalry

<u>1847</u> "It may be, too, that such pursuits belong to *woman's chivalry*, in which she accomplishes tender victories, and with silken cords leads into bondage the stouter heart of man. Happy triumph: in which there is equal delight to the victor and the vanquished."

<u>1924</u> "There are poems of the human soul cut off from God by its loveleasness — the hell of separation of the finite self from the infinite; poems of the "white flame" of a greater love; *woman's chivalry* towards woman ; *woman's chivalry* towards man: and in the end, peace."

<u>1936</u> "Neuilly, but something — perhaps a *woman's chivalry* to another woman — prevented her from doing it."

Chivalric female

<u>1864</u> "The order of Sisters of Charity, therefore, as constituted by St. Vincent de Paul, and whose deeds are known to the whole world, may be considered an aristocratic or *chivalric female* army of volunteers of charity, bound to short terms of service, but generally renewing their vows, and performing prodigies of usefulness."

Chivalrous women

<u>1857</u> "It must be confessed that the spectacle of those three *chivalrous women*, so magnanimous in face of an evil cause… preparing to plunge into the medley of battle, instead of remaining at a distance to watch the fortune of the fray, instead too of shutting themselves up in some luxurious dwelling there to await the intelligence of the result – but armed and mounted – with martial plumes waving over their heads, fire in their eyes and decision on their lips… could have no other effect than the most inspiring one over those who beheld it."

<u>1896</u> "For a lady is among other things a woman with a sense of chivalry, and a *chivalrous woman* uses her finer gifts to supplement the blunt honesty of her husband (if she is the happy possessor of an honest husband)."

<u>1904</u> "The self-sacrificing *chivalrous woman*, with whom duty is a first consideration."

<u>1906</u> "Those *chivalrous Women* seem to be chosen instruments for the world's betterment—all in the general economy of nature — evidence of growth which sometimes takes us by surprise and makes us sit up and think."

<u>1912</u> "Yes — women can he chivalrous! — women can live and die for a conviction! My terrible confession is made easier by your belief!"

<u>1918</u> "to the free and *chivalrous women* of America."

<u>1919</u> "they called upon the free and *chivalrous women* of America to make these wrongs their own and, in so far as possible, to try to redress them, and to safeguard the future of the race by standing for the independence of historic Armenia."

<u>1920</u> "This mighty work of hospital redemption, now so nearly accomplished in all civilized countries, so appealed to *chivalrous women* that there seemed no end to the stream of incoming probationers."

Chivalric woman

<u>1897</u> "We are glad to know that such a noble and *chivalric woman* has her being among the toilers of the overwrought East End, and trust that her good deeds have not gone unrewarded."

Stripped of the usual gender conventions, romantic chivalry reduces to little more than displays of altruism and generosity toward another human being. With that in mind, the sooner women start extending such "chivalry" toward men and boys, and calling it "chivalry," the sooner we might call relationships reciprocal. Until then we will continue to see male-only chivalry by workers on the gynocentric plantation.

We live in a time now of great safety and convenience, and if relationships are to mean anything going forward they will need to be based on some kind of reciprocal chivalry. Men and women can demonstrate their brands of chivalry differently if they wish, a 'co-chivalry' that can be respectful of similarities or differences as agreed between individual men and women. With that move toward reciprocity the one-sided chivalry that the modern world has been so captivated by can be finally put to death.

Sources:

[1] Matthew D. Hammond, Chris G. Sibley, and Nickola C. Overall, The Allure of Sexism: Psychological Entitlement Fosters Women's Endorsement of Benevolent Sexism Over Time
[2] Eric W. Dolan, Self-entitled women are more likely to endorse benevolent sexism, study finds
[3] Matthew D. Hammond, Chris G. Sibley, and Nickola C. Overall [Ibid]
[4] Ruth Styles, The fickle face of feminism: Women are fine with sexism… as long as it benefits them
[5] Lucrezia Marinella: gynocentrism in 1600, at *gynocentrism.com*
[6] Modesta Pozzo: gynocentrism in 1590, at *gynocentrism.com*

Tradwives, modwives and feminists

There's been a lot of discussion lately on a return to traditional gender roles as a way to reverse the ill effects of feminism. We see it promoted by advocates for traditional gynocentrism, and by those who promote non-gynocentric forms of traditionalism, in which men and women are called to adhere to strict 'gender roles' – eg. he is head of household who goes out and earns the money and protects her, while she makes babies, apple pies, and keeps the house clean. Its what many people refer to as the 'two-spheres doctrine' in which men and women are apportioned sovereignty over different realms – he over the political and social realm, and she over the domestic realm. This, argue the advocates of traditional gender roles, creates a delicate but eminently workable balance that has stood the test of time.

The fantasy of a return to the 'good old days' when men were masculine and chivalrous, and women were feminine and ladylike, has run strong through the manosphere and beyond, whether promoted by Anthony "Dream" Johnson and his traditionalism-promoting convention, or women like Suzanne Venker who specialize in promoting traditional roles for women.

I note Mike Buchanan of J4MB recently posted a link on his blog titled *Tradwives – women who are bucking feminism*, which leads to an article with the byline ''Submitting to my husband like it's 1959': Why I became a #TradWife':

And inevitably, it has become a 'thing' for a woman to actually admit that she wants a role as full-time housewife and mother. It's being called a Tradwife, short for traditional wife, though it was only ever a short-lived tradition for most people... Search the hashtag '#tradwife' on social media and you'll see images of cooked dinners and freshly-baked cakes with captions like, "A woman's place is in the home" or "Trying to be a man is a waste of a woman".
There is a lot to that last statement, just as it is a waste of a man trying to be a woman. As Sweden has discovered, the more you try making men and women the same, the more they will emphasise their differences.[1]

I have also witnessed an occasional media article showcasing a woman who has decided to quit a stressful job to live like a 1950s housewife, insisting she's happy to spend her day cooking and cleaning because 'men should be spoiled by their wives.'

One such story in the UK Daily Mail describes a 30 yr old Oregon woman Katrina Holte as follows;

A woman who was stressed out by her job in a busy payroll department, decided to quit the rat race and also turn back time – deciding to live like a 1950s housewife.

Transforming her suburban home in Hillsborough, Oregon, into a working shrine to the era, Katrina Holte, 30, now loves keeping house for her engineering manager husband, Lars, 28 – cleaning, cooking and making dresses using 1950s patterns.

Spinning vinyl discs by stars of the era like Doris Day, she flits about her business, making sure dinner is on the table when Lars gets in, saying: 'I feel like I'm living how I always wanted to. It's my dream life and my husband shares my vision.

'It is a lot of work. I do tons of dishes, laundry and ironing, but I love it and it's helping to take care of my husband and that makes me really happy.[2]

For most working men its a no-brainer that she would be more happy in a traditional roleplay of that kind. It is, as she points out, much better than working a stressful job as required of men's traditional role.

Whatever the trend for women to become tradwives, it is not the only alternative to feminist prescriptions, and it may not be the 'best' of the available alternatives either.

Here I'd like to introduce the phenomenon of "modwives" – women who have embraced multi-option lives over trad roles, and who allow, nay encourage multi-option lives for their husbands. Of course I just made up the term modwife, but they exist and are possibly also growing in number. Both tradwife and modwife eschew feminism which is geared only to female privilege, and not to partnerships based on reciprocal labor and devotion.

Over 150 years of feminism has bequeathed to women the famed multi-option lives, a sword which shattered the more narrow traditional roles with sure and mighty strokes. But the big question is this; are women today willing to renounce their multi-option lives in favour of single option traditional roles?

I would say not a snowfalke's chance in Hell. And to invite them to do so today can be construed as coercive and even an abusive act. I submit that few women today are going to genuinely trade in multi-option lives for traditional roles, other than a limited few who like the idea of free time and cosplay, and who can rely on husbands to bring home a healthy wage.

This unlikelihood that women will embrace roles of yesteryear with any real commitment leads to another option mentioned above – the modwife. At best, today's multi-option women can invite their men to do same. The modwife's *modus operandi* is based on personal liberty within relationships, extending a true freedom of opportunity to her partner such as society has championed for her, even though it goes without saying that the loaded gun remains in her draw, same as it sits in the draw of the tradwife.

Yet few multi-option women today are willing to extend that multi-option liberty to men, preferring instead to pocket the advantages extended by women's 'liberation' while expecting their boyfriends and husbands to remain in the mismatched role of protector and provider. There are women however, limited in number as they are, who lean toward the model of commensurate liberty for both men and women in relationships — some of them you will recognize among the supporters of the men's rights movement.

That libetarian spirit is usually understood as belonging to the political sphere, but it is accepted by the modwife as a guiding principle in her relationship with men. It emphasizes individual choice, relative autonomy, voluntary association, individual judgement, free will, self-determination, and free labor-sharing arrangements and agreements. In a word; *freedom.*

Applying the concept of freedom to relationships may seem odd, especially when we consider the entrapment traditionally associated with marriage, not to mention the dangers and the restrictions on freedom that come with strict, prescribed gender roles of yesteryear.

Psychologist James Hillman speaks to the topic of freedom in his paper *Marriage, Intimacy, Freedom*:

> *Yet what does the soul want with that word Freedom which sets off such expectations? What sort of preposition accompanies and influences Freedom? Freedom from – from fear, want, and oppression, such as enunciated by the Charter that established that established the United Nations after World War Two? Or is it Freedom of – choice, opportunity and movement, or access to today's political language?*

> *Or, is it Freedom to – to do as I like, to hire whom I want, to tell the boss to shove it, to go where I want, to marry whom I please–freedom of agency in the empowered and recovered adult of therapy?*

> *Or, fourth, is it possibly Freedom in? This seems moronic or oxymoronic, for the fantasy of American, epitomized by Texan, freedom is "Don't fence me in." "In" means within limits or constraints of any place, time, situation, condition, such as the kitchen, in an hour, in a conversation, in a marriage.*

This forth preposition, "in," rather than freedom of, to and from, suggests that the joyful expectation arising from the soul when the bell of freedom rings is nothing other than living fully in the actuality of this or that situation, as it is, which gives to that situation wings, freeing it from a desire to be elsewhere, to escape from it, to want more, thereby sating the soul's desire with the fullness of the present. How do I say it "I love what I'm doing... I'm fully in it." "I'm really into tex-mex cooking; my new computer; re-painting the house."[3]

Freedom 'in' as Hillman puts it, allows for creative negotiation on how to set up relationships that bypass the narrow choice-dichotomy between traditional relationships and feminist-informed ones.[*] For example, a man wishes to cook the food or be a stay-at-home father? So be it. She wants a career? Done. A bit of role sharing with him and her — both taking on part-time childcare, cooking and wage earning? Consider it done. This is the kind of freedom that comes with the multi-option couple, and it stands as a viable alternative to the traditional roles that we so often look back to with nostalgia.

The message of the men's rights movement has been consistent in its commitment to more options for men and boys. That call for more options, for more rights and privileges, turns out to be a good match for the liberties most women enjoy today. Whether we use that freedom to choose life with a tradwife or a modwife – or to reject wives and relationships with women completely – the choice is ultimately ours.

References:

[1] *Tradwives – women who are bucking feminism*, J4MB (Jan 2019)
[2] Siofra Brennan, *Woman quits her stressful job to live like a 1950s housewife*, UK Daily Mail (2019)
[3] James Hillman, *Marriage, Intimacy Freedom*, Spring Journal of Archetype and Culture (1997)

*Note: The terms Tradwife and Modwife – and by extension Tradhusband and Modhusband are used in a lighthearted way to designate the different ways people can set up a relationship. Following on from that its probably relevant to give a name to the third area which is dominated by feminist thinking – the one that insists the woman or wife should set the tempo of all relationship matters and the man should simply fall into line instead of mansplaining etc. these can be called the Gynowife & Gynohusband who has no will of his own. By contrast, Tradhusbands and Modhusbands don't need to defer to wives on all matters – they have some agency. Agency – options for and during the relationship, is the central point.

The end of feminism – a prophetic fiction

Many have read Orwell's prophetic book 1984, but few have heard of the 1971 pulp fiction novel The Feminists, an equally prophetic work detailing events that have unfolded -and continue to unfold- in the area of gender politics. Set in the year 1992, the story recounts the rise of misandry and feminist governance that saw women in charge of every detail of civilization, and of a growing resistance movement (to feminism) that mirrors the backlash of antifeminist groups today.

The story tells of how one resistance group, while living in a network of secret underground tunnels, plans and executes a successful bombing at a public gathering attended by both the feminist President and a local Mayor named Verna. The deed is one of many attempts to undermine feminist governance and hasten the end of misandric culture.

During the bombing the feminist President is injured. From a hospital bed she organizes an emergency meeting with executive members of her government, including her old friend and Mayor, Verna, who was witness to the bombing. The following is the pivotal scene in which the President addresses her guests, and where she makes the intriguing suggestion that an increase in female antifeminists has made it impossible for feminist governance to continue.

Here's a summary from the back cover, followed by an excerpt from the end of the book:

THE STORY THAT HAD TO BE WRITTEN—SO TIMELY, SO FRIGHTENINGLY POSSIBLE, YOU WON'T BELIEVE IT'S FICTION!

Take a look into the future…women now rule the world—or most of what's left of it—and their world is not a pretty place to live in. Men have been reduced to mere chattel, good only for procreation. THE FEMINISTS are working to eliminate even this strictly male function…

Men must get permission to make love to any female—even if she is willing—or the penalty is death!

Follow one man's story as he is hunted for just such a crime. In desperation, he stumbles upon the hide-out of the subterranean people—others, like himself—both male and female—who have broken the law of THE FEMINISTS. Hiding in abandoned subway undergrounds, this group of gallant and desperate people wage a guerilla war to overthrow their enslavers.

Excerpt from the book:

The president glanced from one to the other of the women, her eyes finally settling on Verna and softening as if she was remembering their long years of friendship during the rise to power. She smiled weakly and then fixed her gaze on her own hands. There was a look of defeat on her face.

"It has been the policy of our administration to conceal the unfavorable aspect of Feminist control," she said, her voice almost a monotone. "I've spoken to some of you individually about the resistance in Los Angeles and Chicago."

"The pigs can be overcome," the Secretary of Defense interrupted. "We beat them once, we can do it again!"

"No," the president said firmly. "We won't beat them again. We are no longer merely fighting the male element of society. An increasing number of females have joined forces with the men.

"Traitors!"

The president lifted her head and stared at the Secretary of Defense coldly. "This country," she said, "is in the midst of a revolution like it has never known. The only thing keeping us from being ousted is the lack of communication. If the revolutionists in each city did not think they were fighting alone, they would be in control. Fortunately we've dissected the country by cutting off all forms of communication." She met Verna's stunned face. "The resistance movement in New York has been minor in comparison," she said. "But all these groups will soon unite. It's inevitable."

The Mayor, feeling her legs growing weak, turned and sank into a chair.

"The time has come for us to objectively examine our control," the President said. "Unless we return the rights to males that make them equals, our country will be torn apart."

"But they're not equals!" the Secretary of Defense insisted.

"Thirty percent of the female population has suddenly decided they are, " the President said. "To retain control we would be fighting our own sex." She closed her eyes and sighed wearily. "In short," she said, "we must face the fact that Feminist control has failed."

The mayor felt as if she had been struck. "Then it's all been in vain," she mumbled.

"Not entirely," the President told her. "Not if we concede now. Unless we allow ourselves to be beaten and forced into male servitude, we can maintain our dignity. Remember, I said *equals*. In the future, men will consider us in higher esteem. Many of the changes we have brought about will remain in effect. Our control, even though only temporary, has proven that our sex does not make us inferior. "

"Is this what you intend to tell the public?"

"It is."

"You will create mass hysteria."

"I don't think so," the President said. "Granted, there will always be a segment that will resent my decision to reunite the sexes. I suppose there will be guerilla fighters who refuse to comply, but they will be a minority. I only hope none of you are among them. There are many problems our country must face once the question of sexual superiority is conquered. All of us are needed. We must rebuild our environment and stop starvation."

With that scenario fresh in our imagination I leave the reader to decide whether a dramatic increase in female antifeminists – which is now taking place in the real world – will have the effect of reducing the influence and power of feminism.

Recent signs point to a decline of support for feminism, at least in terms of its acceptance by mainstream culture which has become noticeably antifeminist in recent years. Whether it can be replaced by a more compassionate culture of human valorisation and of male~female reciprocity is anyone's guess, but if we are ever to reach that goal it will not come by enforcing a sexist version of chivalry, nor will it come by keeping women high on pedestals.

Source: *The Feminists*, by Parley J. Cooper (pp. 173-75) Pinnacle Books, 1971

Made in United States
Orlando, FL
23 July 2024

49382024R00081